Caterina Benincasa, Gianfranco Neri, Michele Trim
Art and Economics in the City

CW00516296

Urban Studies

Caterina Benincasa, art historian, is founder of Polyhedra (a nonprofit organization focused on the relationship between art and science) and of the Innovate Heritage project aimed at a wide exchange of ideas and experience among scholars, artists and pratictioners. She lives in Berlin.

Gianfranco Neri, architect, teaches Architectural and Urban Composition at Reggio Calabria "Mediterranea" University, where he directs the Department of Art and Territory. He extensively publishes books and articles on issues related to architectural projects. In 2005 he has been awarded the first prize in the international competition for a nursery in Rome.

Michele Trimarchi (PhD), economist, teaches Public Economics (Catanzaro) and Cultural Economics (Bologna). He coordinates the Lateral Thinking Lab (IED Rome), is member of the editoral board of Creative Industries Journal and of the international council of the Creative Industries Federation.

CATERINA BENINCASA, GIANFRANCO NERI,
MICHELE TRIMARCHI (EDS.)

Art and Economics in the City

New Cultural Maps

[transcript]

Bibliographic information published by the Deutsche Nationalbibliothek

The Deutsche Nationalbibliothek lists this publication in the Deutsche Nationalbibliografie; detailed bibliographic data are available in the Internet at http://dnb.d-nb.de

© 2019 transcript Verlag, Bielefeld

Cover layout: Maria Arndt, Bielefeld
Cover illustration: Michele Trimarchi, Rome, 2016
Typeset by Mark-Sebastian Schneider, Bielefeld

Print-ISBN 978-3-8376-4214-8
PDF-ISBN 978-3-8394-4214-2
https://doi.org/10.14361/9783839442142

Content

FOREWORD

Pasquale Catanoso,
Chancellor of the Mediterranea University of Reggio Calabria

Art and economics may appear reciprocally stranger, and somewhat conflictual. History clearly shows that the development of art has always responded to the need for identity on the part of communities sharing values, beliefs and desires in every part of the world. Such a delicate and powerful representation of a common self has grown in the urban fabric, supported by institutional investments and generating diffused richness and well-being.

Not only we owe much of our complex identity to the centrality of Pericle's Athens, Medici's Florence, many Popes' Rome, but also small towns have been the cradle for creativity, ideas, views, and the market for exchanging artefacts, artworks and masterpieces. In such a way the urban fabric is the material and symbolic infrastructure in which the local identity is being consolidated and shared, and at the same time travellers, pilgrims and adventurers have fertilized local identity with their visions.

In a period in which the economic, social and economic paradigm is radically changing, substituting the tired and often abused serial manufacturing system with an unpredictable world where connections, hybridations and a new cooperative orientation will presumably prevail in the value hierarchy, hosting a critical and multi-disciplinary debate on how art and economics can represent a consistent frontier for growth and welfare in the urban framework where intensive flows of ideas, resources and talents will converge in the next years, establishes a dialogue with the spirit of time.

The University of Reggio Calabria adopted the label Mediterranea in order for our unique past, where knowledge was crafted for centuries, to sustain a credible future made of hybridations and creativity. The debate on art, economics and the city presented in this book effectively fulfils our 'third mission': to adopt, valorize and apply knowledge to the social, cultural and economic development of society. The complexity of the current years and the crucial position between the Mediterranean basin and the European continent gives the University of Reggio Calabria the opportunity to play a significant maieutic role, encouraging critical discussion and intensive reaseach.

Many scholars took part in the debate hosted in Reggio Calabria, with the ambition of emphasizing the need for reciprocal listening, interdisciplinary elaborations and versatile projects. Not only different professionals and experts have been involved in the debate: architects, urbanists, philosophers, economists, sociologists; but also an inter-generational exchange of intuitions and experiences makes the book a stimulating synopsis of a wide spectrum of issues, controversies and interpretations. The Mediterranea University is proud of such a rich elaboration, and is firmly oriented towards further challenges for dense debate and valuable research.

INTRODUCTION: URBAN CHALLENGES, CULTURAL STRATEGIES, SOCIAL VALUES

Caterina Benincasa, Gianfranco Neri and Michele Trimarchi

Culture, society and the economy are rapidly changing. Such a radical move from the manufacturing paradigm to some unknown order may prove unexpected and somewhat challenging: for more than two centuries we have all been trained and convinced that the golden age had been attained forever with a few solid certainties such as representative democracy, dimensional happiness, valuable finance, granted peace.

A more careful exploration could reveal some uncomfortable discoveries. Inequalities have grown, democracies are often tired and not sufficiently fed only by the electoral rites; towns have expanded in uncontrolled way generating symmetrical phenomena such as gentrification and social exclusion; finance is crushing the real economy and urbanity; culture itself has been drained into a list of unique objects devoted either to individual possession or to mass tourism. It is time to draw a different map of the city.

Although the urban fabric has always been the cradle for creativity, production of contents, fertilization of know-how and visionary intuitions, elaboration and exchange of ideas, the last centuries seem to have solidified urban dynamics, gradually losing the opportunity to encourage and facilitate the emersion of new social and cultural horizons: the economy and its financial orbit did not admit exceptions, and ended up eliciting pro-active resilience, creative subversion, shared dissent.

A weakened paradigm should not be substituted by a different (but similarly rigid) order. What contemporary society desires is a smooth, permeable, versatile and flexible urban backbone where flows of ideas, contents and experiences can reciprocally fertilize, space can be inclusive, time can be managed. The city of the years to come can generate value out of a moving community and its cultural hybridations, philosophical complexities, shared actions and institutional participation.

This book focuses upon (some of) the many issues arising from the change occurring in our time, and the related need to reshape urban life, overcoming the comfortable framework where functional and symbolic dynamics are driven by the dominating economic and the financial paradigm with its fallout of new inequalities, social rigidities, uneven care. In many respects the convergence towards big cities not only spoiled many small and medium towns but also altered the rythms of ordinary urban life.

Crafted and drafted by an interdisciplinary group of scholars, academics, and professionals active in various areas, this book combines experiences and visions of different generations, in the awareness – often made invisible by frequent intergenerational conflicts – that new cultural maps require pluralism and eclectism, rather than simply rejecting the existing framework in favour of a new hierarchical grid. Over-regulation, symbolic implications, and institutional neglect can only elicit subversive reactions.

The centrality of cities should therefore be regained through new awareness: the rich and often controversial interaction of the analogic and digital dimensions started to generate a counter-flow of professionals going back to smaller and smoother towns, or even moving as digital nomads, the *clerici vagantes* 2.0. In such a framework the ability to redefine urban trails, human networks and social chains proves crucial for each town to effectively respond to the complex need for an eloquent representation of the self.

Art becomes essential not only in providing the urban infrastructure with a powerful language, but also to define the poles for social aggregation, where the formal identity generated by public art is fed by the evolutionary identity of a multicultural community. The value of public art as a powerful tool for urban strategies is focused upon from different perspectives by *Irene Litardi and Lavinia Pastore* (urban management), *Valeria Morea* (public economics), and *Tom Rankin* (architecture). This implies new responsibilities for municipal administrators who need to orientate regulation and public action to material and symbolic dynamics whose trend is partially unpredictable.

Meanwhile, on the background, triggered by basic needs and sophisticated desires new forms of participation in social processes are being crafted, and at the same time the interests of some developers exploit the uncertainties on estate rules and constraints, as *Clarissa Pelino* emphasizes, analyzing the recent contradictions of Mumbai. Exercises of inclusion and integration aim at crafting lively communities; lost jobs and local traditions are being revived or recycled, as in the Riace experience examined by *Domenica Moscato*; tourism faces the gradually growing trade-off between passive masses and versatile voyagers in a wider spectrum of territorial storytelling, as highlighted by *Ottavio Amaro and Marina Tornatora*, and of technological options, as explored by *Arthur Clay and Monika Rut*.

Within such a complex framework in motion there is no neat answer. "Art, Economics and the City" puts forth some of the questions that can allow us to focus upon the present picture and possibly to work from the perspective of various disciplines in order for consistent, effective and sustainable trails to be started. The thesis – and the working hypothesis for forthcoming research – is that it is time for art to move from the ivory towers in which it has complacently been isolated.

This challenge requires a sharper view of the eloquence of the arts and culture as symptoms and cascades of social evolution and turbulence; this can be made possible by projects and policies being grounded on the basis of the exisisting practices as the *mise-en-scène* of needs and desires, whose dynamics are examined by *Lia Fassari* from the sociological perspective; the geography of art, with its unconventional orientations, is tackled by *Federica Antonucci* through the options of de-accessioning and re-location.

In such a way the urban palimpsest can be redrawn, as suggested by *Lidia Errante* in her analysis, due to the proliferation of oriented practices. Urban commons emerge as a response to neglect and dispossession, driven by the desire to claim back urban resources and social cohesion, care and shared responsibility, within the complex, and often conflictual, framework discussed by *Verena Lenna and Michele Trimarchi*.

The book focuses upon these issues, offering technical and critical analyses of a major stage of transition, characterized by ambiguities and contradictions, but also by the sharp potential towards the reclamation of art as a natural part of our *modus vivendi*. It is a complex phenomenon, whose horizons will contribute to shape the society in the next years. Awareness and knowledge are hence strongly needed in order for the diffused fear and mistrust to be offset by constructive views and responsible actions.

This publication has been made possible thanks to the efforts of the University Mediterranea of Reggio Calabria and the Department dArTe - Architecture and Territory, where the conference was held in the framework of the "Innovate Heritage" project. The editors and authors are grateful to the many professionals, academics, students and friends who contributed to our common venture.

1. URBAN STRATEGIES AND SOCIAL DYNAMICS

DOES PUBLIC ART MATTER?
A SOCRATIC EXPLORATION

Irene Litardi and Lavinia Pastore

1. Public art: an exploration

Interventions on urban texture focused on art are often defined 'public art'. Their approach, strategy and shape is widely varied since it depends upon a unique dialogue between an artist and a specific site or area. The label itself cannot lead to a conventional model as it used to be at its beginning when public art was a list of equestrian statues in public squares, aimed at celebrating national or local heroes, or – before that – to remind subjects of the power of the sovereign. Among the several possible definitions a synthetic identification of the features of public art emphasizes its narrative action upon people, describing "the moment when the individual connects herself/himself to the collectively, and the new forms of living together, socialisation, but also homologation, solitude, isolation"[1]. In such an ambiguous and versatile definition we can find the role of the diffused bronze and marble works, public art whose publicness simply lies in its granted visibility to a wide urban community to convey the political value hierarchy of a place.

Since the beginning of history public art has been expression of the dominant power with specific functions:

---

1   Scardi, G. (2011: 18).

1. Decorative – this is a transverse function that characterized every public artwork;
2. Celebrative – usually of power (political or religious) either to reinforce an old power or to establish a new one;
3. Narrative/educational – public art was a tool to tell stories to people and to educate them through images;
4. Functional – public art has been also developed in spaces that had primarily another function (for example bridges, fountains, aqueducts and so on).

Figure 1. Ara Pacis Augustea, 9 a.c – Function: celebrative (of the new power from Republic to Empire).

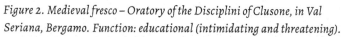

Figure 2. Medieval fresco – Oratory of the Disciplini of Clusone, in Val Seriana, Bergamo. Function: educational (intimidating and threatening).

Figure 3. Barcaccia fountain, Rome – Function: decorative and functional

After the many transformations of the Short Century everything changed and public art was given a different role: that of a shared critical representation of the collective self through non-conventional creative language, made of not necessarily noble materials and the focus upon its impact upon society as a new interpretation of the place and its dynamics with the more complex urban palimpsest.

Figure 4. Statue of Giuseppe Mazzini in Piazza del Duomo, Prato. Function: celebrative (create new identity of Italy as a nation)

Public art may play various roles. Looking at the past we should consider that in many periods artworks were not located in special places but almost evenly spread in the urban grid, until the manufacturing paradigm required a different and more functional shape for towns where the separation between centre and periphery was binary. Such a new shape induced public art to be crafted and located in symbolic places: its role as institutional decoration successfully pursued the goal of maintaining the political, social and possibly cultural status quo. In some cases, public art expands its scope and establishes a creative dialogue with other buildings and monuments in order for institutional messages to be clear and shared, as happened in Italy during the early Fascism years[2]. This is the reason why statues are normally destroyed as soon as a revolution seems to work; it is a declared refusal of the past order, performing a ritually and materially irreversible destruction of its main symbol (the dictator's body, see Figure 5). It belongs to a wider process of *damnatio memoriae*.

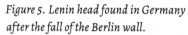

Figure 5. Lenin head found in Germany after the fall of the Berlin wall.

The gradual emersion of a more complex economic and social paradigm is exerting a powerful impact upon the urban dynamics, overcoming the reciprocal indifference between wealthy and poor areas. When artists move to new districts spacial equilibria change. This may elicit reactions such as gentrification, but the speed and intensity of this process appear to be much faster than the establishment's pace. Public art cannot anymore assess the institutional role of urban poles, rather it needs to interpret the balance among urban areas, and aims at exerting an impact upon their social endowment, and visitors' search for local identity. It strengthens the community's sense of belonging, contributes to the increase of quality of urban life, facilitates social inclusion and encourages the (selective) attraction of new residents. This delicate and unique role requires a consistent dialogue between artworks and their site (i.e. the everyday life of their community): stranger art fails, and may emphasize conflictual atmospheres through a

2 See, for a wide discussion on the changing roles of public art, Morea (2018).

clearer perception of urban diseases such as insufficient services, micro-crime, and distance from the places of shared sociality.

The question is not therefore related to the kind of artwork. This is a relevant issue for its semantic power, and its choice is out of the authors' disciplinary realm. Whatever artistic orientation, the challenge with present public art projects is the appropriate and consistent management of the urban area where public art is located. In such a way its presence acts as an attractor and above all as a clearly visible mirror for the urban community: it is not by chance that a powerful work of public art is the giant chrome bean by Anish Kapoor reflecting the everyday stroll in a wide square in Chicago, see Figure 6. This implies a delicate attention on the part of local administration, in order for public art to encourage the intensification of sociality, exchanges, new actions, trade localisation, and the varied activities whose combined occurrence can enhance local growth. No more public since visible, public art in the present is such for its ability to act as a powerful leverage for urban development in a systematic and possibly sustainable way. This requires a synergic strategy on the part of many various institutions, organisations, economic actors, creative artists, social groups and families.

Figure 6. "Cloud Gate", giant chrome bean by Anish Kapoor, Chicago – Function: interaction with the community – The artwork is the mirror of the community.

2. Research approaches

The research starts from a theoretical analysis elaborated on the four main urban change processes: regeneration, requalification, gentrification and self-made urbanism (Peck 2005; Evans and Shaw 2004; Smith 2002; Borri 1985; Glass 1964) and the pioneers who enabled these processes. However, the purpose of the research is to analyse which kind of public art model has been created in the urban change process, and in the specific case of "Triumphs and Laments" in Rome and "Superkilen" in Copenhagen.

The authors carried out ad hoc interviews (Kvale 1996) to the 'pioneers' on cultural processes and experiences in the studied areas. The aim was understanding the story behind a participant's experiences (McNamara 1999), the impact of cultural heritage in regeneration projects, and what is the role of Public Administration to promote these changes. In particular, the interview contains 20 questions:

- questions 1 and 2 are general information of the interviewed;
- questions number 3, 4, 5 and 6 are general questions on the cultural project;
- questions number 7, 8, 9, and 10 are specific questions on the role of the project in the community and territory;
- questions 11, 12 and 13 are focused on the role of urban stakeholders;
- the last questions (from 14 to 20) are based on the role of Public Administration in the project and territory and the future of the project and urban areas in following years.

This stage took one year; the same open-ended questions were asked to all the interviewees; this approach facilitates faster interviews that can be more easily analysed and compared.

The case studies (section 3) was carried out in the Trastevere and Nørrebro neighbourhoods respectively in Rome and in Copenhagen, based on an ethnographic approach for understanding how organizations has undergone changes (Peltonen, 2010). This research process has been held in a participatory context: most of the participants were interested and motivated in the analysis of the urban changing processes that they had contributed to raise and therefore very inclined to give their contribution. The main outcomes of the analysis show a substantial connection between the kind of action carried out and the possible degree of social engagement, along with the shared perception of common profiles in cultural resources. The need to activate cultural investments within a strategic framework, and the symmetrical weakness of occasional action was emphasized. The case studies are enriched by a qualitative research methodology as documental analysis for reviewing and evaluating digital documents (Bowen 2009) and interviews to stakeholders that follow the structure above explained. During the research the information have been systematized, summarized and elaborated in order to present a map of the use and interpretation of unprecedented territorial initiatives and their critical reading on the basis of the main theories and models considered.

3. Case studies

3.1   Triumphs and Laments in Rome: how a wall became a landscape

Between April and June 2016 an Italian water site was the venue – and the object – of a unique art experience: in Roma, along the Tiber River and between the "Sisto" and "Mazzini" bridges, Willliam Kentridge disclosed a 90-metres long frieze devoted to Roman history and chronicle. Its name, "Triumphs and Laments", simply depicts the waves of success and crisis whereby Rome has been continuously driven through the centuries, starting with the she-wolf feeding the Founder Romulus and ending with Pier Paolo Pasolini being brutally killed in the suburbs. The strategic framework of such an unconventional mural (crafted just through the elimination of the dirt from the walls with a cold-water beam) represents a reconciliation between the river and the town, after more than 150 years of reciprocal indifference due to the high walls built by the unitary government after 1870, visually and symbolically separating the Tiber and Rome.

Figure 7. "Triumphs and Laments" frieze by William Kentridge.

"Triumphs and Laments" is a large-scale, 500 meter-long frieze, erased from the biological patina on the travertine embankment walls that line Rome's urban waterfront. Exploring dominant tensions in the history of the Eternal City from past to present, a procession of figures, up to 10 meters high, represents Rome's greatest victories and defeats from mythological to present time, forming a silhouetted procession on Piazza Tevere, how the embankment between Ponte Sisto and Ponte Mazzini is informally defined.

The work was inaugurated on April 21, 2016 with the premiere of a theatrical event created in collaboration with the composer Philip Miller, featuring a live shadow play and two processional bands performing against the backdrop of the frieze. The function of this public art project is narrative and gives the opportunity to regain a part of the city's identity and to influence the transformation of public space, beginning with the adoption of Piazza Tevere. In fact, a diverse team of both Italian and international volunteers, universities, academies, local and foreign institutions has shown enormous interest and generosity in donating and volunteering for a project that speaks of Rome and its history. More than 200 volunteers were involved in the project.

Figure 8. Area of intervention.

Figure 9. "Triumphs and Laments",
opening event.

The innovation of this project lies in its transience. The frieze is going to disappear in a few years, according to its conception on the part of Kentridge: the artwork is transitory like our presence. The function of

"Triumphs and Laments" is not only decorative and narrative but it attracts the attention to the state of degradation of the Tiber.

Figure 10. Detail of the intervention.

3.2   The Superkilen, Copenhagen. A park becomes a space for cultural integration

"Superkilen"[3] is an urban public space wedging through one of the most ethnically diverse and socially challenged neighborhoods in Denmark, Nørrebro[4]. "Superkilen" is a public project promoted by Copenhagen Municipality in partnership with Realdania[5]. The mission through "Superkilen" is to improve multicultural integration and a better urban life style, and to reduce acts of violence and micro-criminality thanks to the co-design of green, sports and social areas in an abandoned area situated not in the city centre although close to it.

---

3 The meaning of "Superkilen" in Danish is "super wedge".

4 Nørrebro is one of the 10 official districts of Copenhagen, Denmark. It is northwest of the city centre.

5 Realdania is a private association active in Denmark, supporting philanthropic projects in the areas of architecture and planning.

Figure 11. Copenhagen' Districts map.

The project was designed thanks to the collaboration between the arts group Superflex, Bjarke Ingels Group (BIG is a Danish architecture and design firm) and Topotek1, a German landscape architecture firm; the park was officially opened in June 2012 after three years of work. The three designers have reacted with the idea of moving here stories and cities from around the world. Through newspapers, radio, internet, electronic mail or install-on-site, they asked residents to suggest urban furnishings for the future Superkilen: each of the 57 ethnic Nørrebro communities could be represented in a park by at least one object. Bjarke Ingels (Founding Partner, BIG, 2012) observed that "rather than a public outreach process towards the lowest common denominator or a politically correct post-rationalization of preconceived ideas navigated around any potential public resistance, we proposed public participation as the driving force of the design leading towards the maximum freedom of expression. By transforming public procedure into proactive proposition we curated a park for the people by the people (peer-to-peer design) literally implemented".

Figure 12. Superkilen

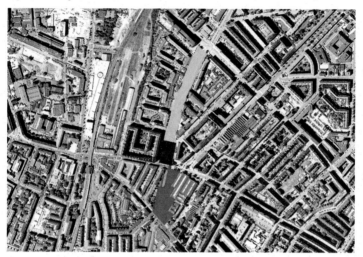

Superliken has one overarching idea that has been conceived as a giant exhibition of urban best practices, a sort of collection of globally found objects coming from the different nationalities of the neighborhood residents. A small stainless plate inlaid in the ground describing it accompanies each object: what it is and where it comes from (in Danish and in the language of its origin). In fact, the "Superkilen" project was co-designed with the residents, asked them what they wanted in a public park from their Countries; The Superflex group observed: "Our mission was to craft the big picture in the extreme detail of a personal memory or story, which on the surface might appear insignificant, but once hunted down and enlarged became super big. A glass of Palestinian soil in a living room in Nørrebro serving as a memory of a lost land, enlarged to a small mountain of Palestinian soil in the park. A distant Mediterranean flirt in the 1970s symbolised by a great iron bull, hunted down and raised on a hill in the park" (Superflex, 2012). The conceptual starting point is a division of "Superkilen" into three zones and colours: green, black and red in 750 metres. The different surfaces and colours were integrated to form new, dynamic surroundings for the everyday objects.

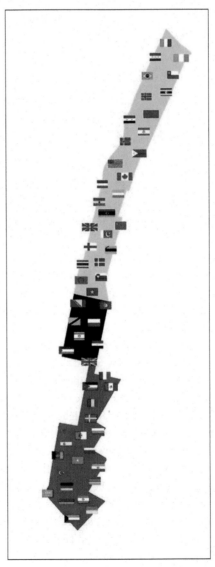

The American Institute of Architects awarded the project with a 2013 AIA Honor Award in the Regional & Urban Design category. It was shortlisted for the Design of the Year award by the Design Museum in London as well as for the European Union Prize for Contemporary Architecture.

4. Concluding remarks

The two case studies presented in this chapter can be useful to carry out a reflection of the initial research questions raised on the role of public art in present time:

Do they represent the community that live there?
Both case studies represent the intention to establish a dialogue with the community living in a wide urban area, but there are two substantial differences between Rome and Copenhagen:

- The intervention in Copenhagen is a coral expression of public art, since many artists from all over the world express creativity. The intervention in Rome is the artwork of a single artist, William Kendrige, who was asked to interpret the relationship between the city, its history and its community.
- The community of reference of the two projects is different. While the "Superkilen" is a multicultural site-specific community of a Copenhagen neighbourhood, the project of Rome addresses a wider community where residents and visitors belong with no tight territorial connection. Indeed, the Tiber river is a sort of urban backbone and the frieze aims at establishing, and possibly consolidating, a dialogue with the complex history of Rome itself on the part of any specific social and territorial groups.

Have we overcome the concept of public art as expression of certain power?
For sure each case study above examined starts from a different perspective about the role of public art, with the idea that it is expression of different communities, through stakeholders involved in the project, and do not express the vision of a single power.

Is public art a new tool for transforming a neighbourhood into the place for a new community?
The attempt of both projects is to intervene in the neighbourhood where they are located and contribute to enhance a sense of community and of belonging through art.

Does the regeneration process starts from a spontaneous artists' intervention that might be transformed afterwards into gentrification?
This specific question is related to the Copenhagen project since in the case of Rome we cannot talk about gentrification of that area of the city. Indeed the area of the Tiber involved in Kentridge's work is located between the historic centre and Trastevere, both areas variably developed (Trastevere already gentrified by other phenomena) but not harmoniously connected with Piazza Tevere. What the intervention in Rome seeks is a new and more intensive attention to the Tiber area that proves quite isolated from the urban flows. Until now the Kendrige work has not changed that situation of neglect, since the attention to that area was temporary and did not achieve continuance. The "Superkilen" experience is too recent to evaluate whether the project may lead to gentrifying the area around it.

Is public art functional and planned by public administrations or private developers who want to invest into certain neighbourhoods?
This interpretation of public art as a tool for Public Administrations and private investors to intervene and change a specific urban area might be true in different contexts but not in the ones analyzed. The behaviour of the PA is quite different in the two case studies:

- "Superkilen" is part of a PA strategy. The Public Administration has to support medium-long term projects and strategies that show an integrated perspective. Indeed, the Public Administration, within a long-term strategy in terms of policies and funds, coordinated Copenhagen's experiences. "Superkilen" is part of a series of projects that have made Copenhagen one of the best practices at the forefront of sustainable cities, elected among the best cities in the world to live and work.
- "Triumphs and Laments" was not funded by the public administration, although the removal of the dirt from the Tiber wall was an in-kind intevention on the part of the waste removal municipal agency. The "Tevereterno" association and other participants promoted the whole process.

For sure, one of the reason why "Triumphs and Laments" achieved a very limited continuity and was not linked to other initiatives is the lack of active support from the PA. The municipal administration of Rome is not pursuing any medium-long term strategies concerning the role and the urban links the Tiber should have in the future of the city. Our case studies clearly demonstrate that the success of an intervention should be based on the regular participation of residents, and on co-design of goods and services aimed at making the area familiar and crowded. The cultural production has to be integrated into the eco-system where it is installed, and its design into its community.

References

Albareda, L./Lozano, J.M./Ysa, T. (2007): "Public Policies on Corporate Social Responsibility: The Role of Governments in Europe". Journal of Business Ethics 74, pp. 391-407.

Alkhafaji, A.F. (1989): A Stakeholder Approach to Corporate Governance: Managing in a Dynamic Environment, Quorum Books.

Atkinson, R. (2004): "The Evidence on the Impact of Gentrification: New Lessons for the Urban Renaissance?". European Journal of Housing Policy 4/1, pp.107-131.

Atkinson, R./Bridge, G. (2005): Gentrification in a Global Context, the New Urban Colonialism, New York: Routledge.

Becker, J. (2014): "Nella Periferia Centrale". In Cellamare C. (ed.), S.M.U.R., Roma città autoprodotta, ricerca urbana e linguaggi artistici, Castel San Petro Romano: Manifestolibri, pp. 121-143.

Belligni, S./Ravazzi, S. (2013): La politica e la città. Regime urbano e classe dirigente a Torino, Bologna: Il Mulino.

Bianchini, F./Parkinson, M. (1993): Cultural Policy and Urban Regeneration: the West European Experience, Manchester: Manchester University Press.

Bishop, Patrick/Davis, Glyn (2002): "Mapping Public Participation in Policy Choices". Australian Journal of Public Administration 61/1, pp. 14-29.

Boniburini, I. (2009): "Le parole della città". In: Boniburini, I. (ed.), Alla ricerca della città vivibile, Firenze: Alinea, pp. 45-58.

Borri, D. (1985): Lessico urbanistico, Bari: Dedalo.

Cameron, S./Doling, J. (1993): "Housing Neighbourhoods and Urban Regeneration". Urban Studies 31/7, pp. 1211-1223.

Cellamare, C. (1999): Culture e progetto del territorio, Milano: Franco Angeli.

Cellamare, C. (2012): Progettualità dell'agire urbano. Processi e pratiche urbane, Roma: Carocci.

De Toni, A.F./Nonino, F. (2009): "La misura del capitale sociale organizzativo attraverso le reti informali". Sviluppo & Organizzazione, pp. 54-67.

De Varine, H. (2005): "Le radici del futuro". In: Jallà, D. (ed.), Il patrimonio culturale al servizio dello sviluppo locale, Bologna: Clueb, pp. 8-9.

Etzkowitz, H./Leydesdorff, L. (2000): "The Dynamics of Innovation: from National Systems and 'Mode 2' to a Triple Helix of University-Industry-Government Relations". Research Policy 29, pp. 109-123.

Evans, G. (2004): "Cultural Industry Quarters". In Bell D./Jayne M. (eds.), City of Quarters: Urban Villages in the Contemporary City, Burlington: Ashgate, pp. 109-130.

Florida, R. (2002): The Rise of the Creative Class: and how it is Transforming Work, Leisure, Community and Everyday Life, New York: Basic Books.

Freeman, R.E. (1984): Strategic Management: A Stakeholder Approach, Boston: Pitman.

Freeman, R.E. et al. (2010): Stakeholder Theory. The State of the Art, Cambridge: Cambridge University Press.

Glass, R. (1964): "Introduction: aspects of change". In: MacGibbon/Kee (eds.), London: aspects of chance, London: Centre for Urban Studies, pp. xiii-xlii.

Jeffrey, N. (2009): Stakeholder Engagement: A Road Map to Meaningful Engagement, Doughty Centre: Cranfield School of Management.

Khazaei, A./Elliot, S./Joppe, M. (2015): "An application of stakeholder theory to advance community participation in tourism planning: the case for engaging immigrants as fringe stakeholders". Journal of Sustainable Tourism 23/7, pp. 1049-1062.

Koch, A./Stahlecker, T. (2006): "Regional Innovation Systems and the Foundation of Knowledge Intensive Business Services. A Comparative Study in Bremen, Munich, and Stuttgart, Germany". European Planning Studies 14/2, pp. 123-146.

Lee, R.L.M. (2005): "Bauman, Lquid Modernity and Dilemmas of Development". Thesis Eleven 83, pp. 61-77.

Lees, L. (2008): Gentrification and Social Mixing: toward an inclusive urban renaissance?. Urban Studies 45/12, pp. 2449-2470.

Litardi, I./Pastore, L./Trimarchi, M. (2016), "Culture and the City. Public Action and Social Participation in Rome's Experience". Journal of Business and Economics 7/7, pp. 1168-1181.

Logan, J.R./Molotch, H. L. (1987): Urban Fortunes: The Political Economy of Place, Los Angeles CA: University of California Press.

Maggi, M. (2002): Ecomusei. Guida europea, Torino: Allemandi.

Mitchel, R. et al (1997): "Toward a Theory of Stakeholder Identification and Salience: Defining the Principle of Who and What Really Counts". Academy of Management Review 22/4, pp. 853-886.

Morad, M. (2008): "Sustainable Communities: a Conceited Metaphor or an Achievable Aim?". Local Economy 23/3, pp. 111-112.

Morea, V. (2018): L'arte pubblica in Italia. Politiche e impatti sul territorio, unpublished manuscript.

Ostrom, E./Hess, C. (2006): Understanding Knowledge as a Commons: From Theory to Practice, Cambridge MA: The MIT Press.

Peck, P. (2005): "Struggling with the Creative Class". International Journal of Urban and Regional Research 29/4, pp. 740-770.

Pogrebin, R. (2009): "Philanthropist with a Sense of Timing Raises Her Profile". The New York Times, June 29th.

Radywyl, N./Biggs, C. (2013): "Reclaiming the Commons for Urban Transformation". Journal of Cleaner Production 50, pp. 159-170.

Ranga, M./Etzkowitz, H. (2013): "Triple Helix Systems: an Analytical Framework for Innovation Policy and Practice in the Knowledge Society". Industry and Higher Education 27/4, pp. 237-262.

Sassen, S. (1997): La città nell'economia globale, Bologna: Il Mulino.

Scardi, G. (2011, ed.): Paesaggio con figura. Arte, sfera e trasformazione sociale, Torino: Allemandi.

Semenza, J./March, T., (2009): "An Urban Community-Based Intervention to Advance Social Interactions". Environment & Behavior 41/1, pp. 22-42.

Smith, N. (1997): The New Urban Frontier: Gentrification and the Revanchist City, London: Routledge.

Smith, N. (2002): "New Globalism, New Urbanism: Gentrification as Global Urban Strategy". Antipode 34/3, pp. 434-457.

Svara, J.H./Denhardt, J. (2010): The Connected Community: Local Governments as Partners in Citizen Engagement and Community Building, Tempe AZ: Arizona State University Press.

Toomey, B. (2008): "Can the Use of Technology Encourage Young People to Take an Active Part in Urban Regeneration Consultations? A Case Study from East London". Local Economy 23/3, pp. 247-251.

Visconti, L. M./Sherry Jr., J.F./Borghini, S./Anderson, L. (2010): "Street Art, Sweet Art? Reclaiming the 'Public' in Public Place". Journal of Consumer Research 37/3, pp. 511-529.

Vivek, N.M. et al. (2007): "Defining, Identifying and Mapping Stakeholders in the Assessment of Urban Sustainability". In: M. Horner M./Hardcastle C./Price A./Bebbington J. (eds.), Whole Life Urban Sustainability and its Assessment, Glasgow: Caledonian University, pp. 54-72.

Warner, M. (2002): "Publics and Counterpublics". Public Culture 14/1, pp. 49-90.

Williams, P./Smith, N. (1986): "From Renaissance to Restructuring: the Dynamics of Contemporary Urban Development". In: Smith N./Williams P. (eds.), Gentrification of the City, Boston: Blackwell, pp. 125-147.

Zukin, S. (2010): Naked city. The Death and Life of Authentic Urban Places, New York NY: Oxford Press.

ART AND TERRITORIAL CHANGES IN THE ITALIAN EXPERIENCE

Valeria Morea

1. The city and its 'creative milieu'

As Hall reminds us, "cities have always been places where human creativity flourished" (Hall, 2009: 49) fostering the greatest art but also the most advanced thoughts, technological inventions, industries and markets. Cities indeed grow in scale, population, economic power, and become the place of innovative solutions to great urban management problem. Hall then distinguishes four kinds of urban innovation: cultural/intellectual; technological/productive; cultural/technological; technological/organisational. In the end, the author forecasts a merge of the four during the twenty-first Century. Patterns of development of such cities can be quite unclear or characterised by unexpected or emerging factors, but a few recurring elements can be found.

Cities become creative because of their 'creative milieu'. This statement hints at clarifying that creativity is an intangible factor of success. Even when we talk about cities shaped by artists, the key is not just the artifact, but the shared knowledge itself (Tornqvist, 2004). A creative milieu in nurtured by exchange of people. Creatively rising cities become an attraction for talents and capitals. Notwithstanding, "the physical *milieu*'s continuity makes it an important historical source" (Tornqvist, 2004: 232). In order for a process of urban renewal and for its creative attractiveness to flourish, "even the architecture of a city's buildings, as well as their interior decoration and colours, are thought to have a certain importance" (Tornqvist, 2004: 232).

A situation of instability is necessary for the development of a creative milieu. Hence, an "unstable phase characterized by stagnation and confusion" (Tornqvist, 2004: 234) is the phase in which ideas start conflicting and original creative people converging. Also, a previous situation of wealth – that could match Tornqvist's *stable phase* (Tornqvist, 2004) – positively affects the rise of a creative city. Hall states that creative cities were *bourgeois* cities – but *bourgeois* cities were not necessarily creative. Here, culture was prompted by a minority of people and wealth was unequally distributed[1].

Such a duality can lead to several risks and misunderstandings but a synthesis of these two factors can still be offered. Following Hall's assertion, talent is considered more important than wealth and, in the end, wealth must be considered as a means towards long-term cultural benefits. This is the most misunderstood point. Openness is therefore a basic factor of success for cities which prove open when they accept migrations of talents and knowledge. Through history, an oligarchic patronage of creativity[2] lets artists shape cities and their environment. Such a process results not only in urban landscape's significant changes but also in quality of urban life and urban atmosphere.

Today, cities compete for liveliness and quality of life (Hall, 1998, Richards and Palmer, 2010). They struggle to be attractive for workers, residents and tourists. In this light, attraction of talents and tolerance as, for instance, Florida puts in his writings, should be interpreted in a reverse way. Florida (2002) argues that creative classes are instrumental to economic development and innovation of the city. Comparing this perspective to Hall's, it rather seems arguable that a sound economic basis is a means for creativity to emerge and quality of life to increase. This said, the arts offer cities a range of impacts that is much

---

1 An interesting cue is given by sociologist Bourdieu, who argues that social and family conditions are largely responsible for individual disposition to cultural consumption and the definition of aesthetic taste (Bourdieu, 1989).
2 For instance, Florence with de' Medici and Rome with the Popes.

broader than the mere economic development, and their role is instrumental to wellbeing and happiness of people[3].

2. Public places

What we are talking about is public benefit: the arts deserve to be publicly underpinned and offered to the public, that is the urban community (Matarasso, 2004). Moreover, even if the intangible nature of creative milieu has previously been marked as essential, its material component shows a remarkable importance in the development of a creative city. Proximity is a basic factor in territorial development and this is still true in the cultural realm. For instance, cultural and creative exchanges used to take places in *piazza*, *agora* or cafés. These public places played a key public and social role.

As the reader might have noticed, the term "public" has been mentioned in this sentence many times with many different meanings. Public space, public intervention, the public, public art, all these *publics* refer to different stakeholders[4] that, all together and mutually interconnected, constitute the territory.

Public spaces of cities are the places where non codified relations and connections occur. They are used or at least crossed by the whole urban population, with little or no distinction related to social differences. Hence, public space can be the perfect scene of a non-prejudicial and fruitful experience of the arts, with no threshold dividing people from art consumption. In this respect, public space is better defined with the term 'public realm' (Lavanga and Pastorino, 2006). This im-

---

3 Recently Professor Marie Briguglio exposed her findings about quality of life and cultural participation at Valletta 2018 Fouth International Conference "Living Cities, Liveable Spaces: placemaking and Identity", 22-24 November 2017 La Valletta, Malta https://newsmavens.com/news/women-to-watch/924/economist-marie-briguglio-culturally-active-citizens-are-happier (website consulted on Jan 2018)

4 An interesting insight on the stakeholders view is offered by Moore and Khagram (2004).

plies that art in urban public spaces could be the place where democratisation of culture can actually be applied. People crossing and acting within the public realm are the public and at the same time art consumers, addressees and funders of public policies and interventions.

Then, art in the public realm (*i.e.* public art) is to be considered a preferred option in order for cultural borders to become wider, for civic openness to increase and for creative milieu to flourish. Public art is a multi-faceted form of art difficult to be described by one single definition. Seia (2011) observes that the "languages of the arts are mind-trainer and when art is practiced in a public space, out of the unconventional cultural places, it can reach various publics, different truths and new scenarios"[5].

3. Art in public spaces: some experience

Art in public spaces is a powerful means of social transformation. This trend has been underpinned by institutional actions such as the European Capital of Culture program but, as Hall and Robertson (2001) argued almost two decades ago proving right also nowadays, claims of benefits generated by public art still have to be scientifically demonstrated. Such claims concern communities' sense of identity, sense of place, communities' needs and social inclusion, educational values and social change. Furthermore, it is also remarkable that those claims do not take into consideration the intention of the public artwork's author, the artist her/himself. With regard to this point, it can be noted that the artist willing to cope with public art is looking for a "dialogue with a different patron, a new way of exploring the reality and its constraints related to the promoter, who is not simply the collector anymore, but someone who asks for creative interventions for the community" (Detheridge, 2004: 106)[6].

---

5 Translation by the author of this chapter.
6 Translation by the author of this chapter.

Recently, the discourse around what art can do to society is arising and this is getting confirmed by practices such as Public Art Fund's latest exhibition by Chinese refugee artist Ai Weiwei "Good fences make good neighbors"[7]. Also, Public Art Fund states in its own mission to commit to a broad public for free exhibitions and impacting on the urban experience[8]. Similarly does the collective The Federation, whose website resolutely states: "Art is essential to democracy"[9].

Together with increasingly aware statements about the instrumental use of public art, a deeper consciousness around the importance of the role of creativity and art in the cities is rising with evaluation attempts. For instance, a remarkable example of the rising interest for the assessment of the role of art for cities is the "City, Culture and Creativity Monitor" by European Commission[10], an evaluation tool of the European creative cities based on three main pillars: cultural vibrancy; creative economy; enabling atmosphere.

Even if this is not the place for a long dissertation about the experiences of art in public spaces, a glance at a couple of examples is valuable for our purposes. The experiences to be examined are Christo's "Floating Piers" on the Lake Iseo and Kentridge's "Triumphs and Laments" frieze in Rome, both in Italy. "Floating Piers" is an installation by the Bulgarian-American artist Christo that took place in Lake Iseo for two weeks in July 2016. The project has been carried out and totally funded by an *ad hoc* limited liability company founded by Christo himself in Italy. The artist and his team installed a three-kilometres grid of floating docks connecting the three small towns of Lake Iseo (Sulzano, Monte Isola and San Paolo island), normally connected by boat lines, with a pedestrian path. The piers were covered with a vibrant turmeric yellow fabric that turned its shades with daylight and

---

7 https://www.publicartfund.org/ai_weiwei_good_fences_make_good_neighbors (website last visit: Jan 2018)

8 https://www.publicartfund.org/about (website last visit: Jan 2018)

9 https://wearethefederation.org/ (website last visit: Jan 2018)

10 https://composite-indicators.jrc.ec.europa.eu/cultural-creative-cities-monitor/ (website last visit: Jan 2018)

when wet. "Those who experienced the 'Floating Piers' felt like if they were walking on water – or perhaps the back of a whale", said Christo. "The light and water transformed the bright yellow fabric to shades of red and gold throughout the sixteen days"[11]. In the end, the art piece was not just the material piers but the whole value of two weeks of as many experiences as the visitors were[12].

"There were no tickets, no openings, no reservations and no owners. The 'Floating Piers' was an extension of the street and belonged to everyone"[13]. For sixteen days Lake Iseo has been packed with Italian and international visitors who took part of the installation and became part of a new temporary landscape. Even though, such a new landscape proved to be not so temporary. After two weeks the installation was dismantled but the perception of that landscape has changed for visitors and, also, for the socio-economic environment. For instance, one year later tourism was still at peak levels regardless of the "Floating Piers"[14].

The latter experience concerns an art intervention carried out by South African artist William Kentridge along the Tiber river in the heart of Rome. The artwork is a frieze surfaced from the biological coat of river banks walls[15]. The frieze depicts eighty ten metres tall icons of the history and chronicle of the city: a parade of Rome's triumphs and laments, its victories and defeats. Icons have been selected among pictures drawn from history of art, literature, journals and newspapers, movies, monuments and other sources. The elements of the frieze, realized with an environment-friendly technique based on high-pres-

11 http://archive.thefloatingpiers.com/the-project
12 1.2 milions, according to the impact analysis report carried out by JFC: www.jfc.it/ ricerche-istituzionali/christo-the-floating-piers-consuntivo-appraisal
13 http://archive.thefloatingpiers.com/the-project
14 http://www.lastampa.it/2017/06/17/edizioni/milano/sul-miracolo-del-floating-piers-lago-anno-dopo-linstallazione-diseo-christo-visitata-da-milione-turisti-mila-persone-continua-lafflusso-di-ygf8Nj58znQKf54iYhqdxN/pagina.html
15 Cf. Biagioni A., Borriello C., Sassanelli V., *Triumphs and Laments di William Kentridge. Tevereterno per Roma*, Edizione Tevereterno, Roma, 2016

sure cold water cleaning, speak directly to Rome residents and visitors, called to recognise the icons and detect cultural and everyday chronicles recalls. By means of the technique of high-pressure water cleaning on stencil used by Kentridge to let icons emerge from the mosses of the bank walls, the frieze is intended to last for approximately five years. In fact, as no maintenance action has purposely been planned by the artist himself, the mosses will grow again with the result of a gradual maquillage of the figures.

The project has been managed by an Italian cultural nonprofit organisation named Tevereterno, whose mission is to give the banks of Tiber river back to civic usage, through a series of art projects, mostly connected with the foundation date of the ancient Rome (April 21, 753 BC). Kentridge's frieze has been the most ambitious project carried by Tevereterno so far, and it has gained a quite high fortune during its implementation and inauguration. In spite of this, numerous problems with the public administration emerged during the frieze proposal phase[16]. It took several years of negotiation between Tevereterno and the Municipality of Rome in order to gain the necessary permissions for Triumphs and Laments' execution[17]. Moreover, it is notable that the Municipality was not asked to participate in the project financially and all the funding efforts have been carried out by Tevereterno itself, by means of crowdfunding, sponsorships, volunteering. After two years from its inauguration, Kentridge's frieze still struggles to become Roman citizens' frieze, partly due to the weak action of the promoter organization, partly due to a general indifference of administrators towards the project. At this point one main and more general question arises: what can art do for the public places?

---

16 National and local chronicle largely focused on this issue. For instance, cf. Mozzetti C. *Graffiti sul Tevere, il ministero frena*, Il Messaggero, 15 gennaio 2014.

17 Granovetter, M.S. (1973)

4. Conclusions and implications

Some remarks can be drawn from the cases described before, that will lead to an attempt of answering to the aforesaid general question. A first element to be noted is timing. Both the public art experiences described above are temporary. Furthermore, such a feature has a twofold consequence. On the one hand, we find the importance of temporary artistic projects, *i.e.* events, for cities. As Palmer and Richards put it, "cultural events have become central to processes of urban development and revitalisìation, as cultural production becomes a major element of the urban economy, and cultural consumption can dominate both the image of places and urban life in general". Moreover, "[claiming distinction] also involves the creation of a lively atmosphere and a sense of place" (Palmer and Richards, 2010: 3).

Events and temporary engagement produce a deep exchange and interaction among groups because people feel committed to participate and to give their best (Granovetter, 1973). According to that, Christo's action on Lake Iseo can be considered as a very powerful experience. It has produced an explosive (*i.e.* short term) range of benefits to the visitors and also to the socio-economic fabric; indeed, its effects on tourism and local economy have been and still prove to be significant. But the most powerful effect is that the "Floating Piers" experience has systematically changed the perception of the landscape for those who experienced a walk on them and possibly, also, by means of media and social media sharing contents, such a shift in perception might have addressed an even broader audience.

Eventually Lake Iseo, after "Floating Piers" was dismantled, might not have returned to what it was before Christo and people's interaction with that landscape. Still with regard to the temporary nature of the aforementioned artistic events, on the other hand, another feature is to be taken into account: the success of an event with such a promising legacy cannot be taken for granted. This means that together with a short time artistic action, many more interventions need to be provided in order to support the long term legacy the event is charged to offer.

As Palmer and Richards (2010: 432) argue, "the eventful city planning process needs to be integrated with other planning frameworks to ensure that synergies with other policy areas can be maximized, and to enable events to be embedded into the cultural fabric of the city".

In such a respect "Triumphs and Laments" shows some weaknesses. The very powerful aim of Kentridge's frieze was to arise a subtle but increasing territorial change. Everyday life of city users would have been gradually affected by the presence of a very engaging *oeuvre* open to everybody at any time. This would have little by little enabled people to use and take care of that public space that could become public, *i.e.* everybody's, place. Even if it appears to be promising because of its medium-term duration and its stance in re-establishing a portion of public space for its citizens, the lack of embedment in a more general and publicly underpinned strategy for the regeneration of that urban space performed as a failure factor, emphasized by the obstacles brought about by public governance in the implementation phase and by its almost absent interest in the whole project[18].

To conclude, we must acknowledge that public art is not always self-standing. When not accompanied and sustained by other parallel efforts, public art actions can lose in success and prove mediocre in their impacts. Therefore, the lesson to learn seems to be that art alone does not prove sufficient to serve urban regeneration. Wider efforts must be combined in order for a cultural urban strategic project to be successful for people and their city.

References

Biagioni, A./Borriello, C./Sassanelli, V. (2016): Triumphs and Laments di William Kentridge, Roma: Tevereterno.

---

18 Notwithstanding, the frieze is still well visible and the five years have not expired yet. Hopefully, more and better could be done in the near future.

De Luca, M./Gennari Santori, F./Pietromarchi, B./Trimarchi, M. (eds., 2004): Creazione contemporanea. Arte società e territorio tra pubblico e privato, Roma: Sossella.

Detheridge, A. (2004): "Artisti e sfera pubblica", in De Luca, M./Gennari Santori, F./Pietromarchi, B./Trimarchi, M. (eds.): Creazione contemporanea. Arte società e territorio tra pubblico e privato, Roma: Sossella, pp. 105-119.

Florida, R.L. (2002): The rise of the creative class, and how it is transforming work, leisure, community and everyday life, New York: Basic Books.

Granovetter, M.S. (1973): "The strength of weak ties", American Journal of Sociology, 78/6, pp. 1360-1380.

Hall, P. (1998): Cities in Civilization, London: Weidenfield & Nicolson.

Hall, P. (2009): "The Age of the City: the Challenge for Creative Cities", in Giok L.O./Yuen B. (eds.) World Cities: Achieving Liveability and Vibrancy, River Edge NJ: World Scientific Publishing, pp. 47-70.

Hall, T./Robertson, I. (2001): "Public Art and Urban Regeneration: advocacy, claims and critical debates", Landscape Research, 26/1, pp. 5-26.

Lavanga, M./Pastorino, S. (2006): "Arte pubblica e pianificazione urbana nell'esperienza olandese", Economia della Cultura, 16/3, pp. 319-328.

Matarasso, F. (2004): "L'etat, c'est nous: arte, sussidi e stato nei regimi democratici", Economia della Cultura, 16/4, pp. 491-499.

Moore, M./Khagram, S. (2004): "On Creating Public Value. What Business Might Learn from Government about Strategic Management", Corporate Social Responsibility Initiative, 3, pp. 1-24.

Mozzetti, C. (2014): "Graffiti sul Tevere, il ministero frena", Il Messaggero, January 15th.

Richards, G./Palmer, R. (2010): Eventful cities: cultural management and urban revitalization, Oxford: Butterworth-Heinemann.

Scardi G. Ed. (2011): Paesaggio con figura. Arte, sfera pubblica e trasformazione sociale, Torino: Allemandi.

Seia, C. (2011): "Prefazione", in Scardi G. (Ed.) Paesaggio con figura. Arte, sfera pubblica e trasformazione sociale, Torino: Allemandi.

Törnqvist, G. (2004): "Creativity in time and space", Geografiska Annaler, 86/4, pp. 227-243.

Websites

The floating piers (http://archive.thefloatingpiers.com)

"Il miracolo del Floating Piers: un anno dopo Christo i turisti corrono al lago d'Iseo", June 17, 2017 (http://www.lastampa.it/2017/06/17/edizioni/milano/sul-miracolo-del-floating-piers-lago-anno-dopo-linstallazione-diseo-christo-visitata-da-milione-turisti-mila-persone-continua-lafflusso-di-ygf8Nj58znQKf54iYhqdxN/pagina.html)

"Cultural and Creative Cities Monitor", European Commission (https://composite-indicators.jrc.ec.europa.eu/cultural-creative-cities-monitor/)

"Economist Marie Briguglio: culturally active citizens are happier" December 11, 2017 (https://newsmavens.com/news/women-to-watch/9 24/economist-marie-briguglio-culturally-active-citizens-are-happier)

We the federation (https://wearethefederation.org)

Public Art Fund, New York (https://www.publicartfund.org)

JFC Consulting (www.jfc.it)

CULTURE MEETS ECOLOGY IN THE PUBLIC SPACE
'TRIUMPHS AND LAMENTS' ON THE TIBER

Tom Rankin

"Because cities gather together differences, strangers need a center,
they need somewhere to meet and
to interact. But the sheer arousals
of the center are not enough to
create and urban polity; the polity
requires further a place for discipline, focus, and duration."
Richard Sennett (1998)

"There are things we should hold on
to but forget. And historical memories, things that society should remember, that get forgotten."
William Kentridge (2016)

1. Foreword

As Rome rushes forward in its fourth millennium, its ongoing experiment in urban transformation is as riveting as ever. Few cities offer
as rich a spectacle of starts and stops, of sacks, sieges and stagnation
alternating with growth spurts, strategic developments and spon-

taneous expansion. The world's most resilient city, Rome has always found a way to rebuild, but never from scratch.

In today's global urbanization, city-making often means inserting new pieces of architecture, or even complete pieces of city, what Fumihiko Maki called "collective form" (Mayne, 2015 p. 14) especially in urban areas where large tracts are abandoned or devastated by disasters. Even in the Eternal City there is a role for big thinking, for regional strategies, and for projects which address infrastructure as a catalyst for urban regeneration. Roman leaders have imposed collective form onto sites cleared by fires and floods, or in its *disabitato*, tracts of green space abandoned by a shrinking population. Nero rebuilt after the fire of 64 AD with wider, straighter streets, and the Renaissance popes from Julius II to Sixtus V cut axial boulevards through the historic fabric to establish new urban connections. In the twentieth century Mussolini's *sventramenti* scarred the city while gouging out historic fabric and replacing it with over-scaled monumental architecture. And already decades before Fascism, after becoming capital of unified Italy, Roma Capitale saw the radical transformation of its most central historic infrastructure, the Tiber river.

But such bold moves are not the only way to shape cities. Sometimes – and this is true especially in cities like Rome where architecture has had centuries to accrue – urban architects can leverage the existing fabric and artifacts and produce successful urbanism with the most minimal of interventions. This chapter will chronicle one such intervention along Rome's riverfront: the establishment of a new public space dubbed Piazza Tevere and the production of the largest public art project ever produced, "Triumphs and Laments", by artist William Kentridge. My hope is that, using the Kentridge project as a case study, we can better understand how art can serve as a catalyst to spur social change, and how the city can leverage its existing resources to do more with less.

2. The Site

Rome's Tiber Riverfront has not always been the desolate *terrain vague* that presents itself to us today. In 1704 Alessandro Specchi completed the Porto di Ripetta, a bustling baroque *scalinata* descending from the city to its river banks, and inversely welcoming merchants and visitors arriving by boat up into the Campus Martius. Images of the Tiber from this time show lively boat traffic, floating mills, and great numbers of people lounging around the river banks. Fishing and swimming were so popular that they were regulated by papal decree. As Rome's most important economic, environmental, ecological, and recreational re-source, according to architect and Tiber historian, Maria Margarita Segarra Lagunes, the Tiber didn't just run through the city; it was part of the city.

The river would frequently overflow its banks and invade the city streets, as documented in the hydrometer on the wall of the Church of San Rocco, flooding ground floors and filling monuments such as the Pantheon with muddy water. It was hard to ignore the river's fickle presence. The Tiber was both a blessing and a curse. The lifeblood of the city could also prove a menace when heavy rains upstream filled its narrow channels causing it to breach its banks. Reflecting on the eternal city, Henry James wrote of "the sad-looking, evil-looking, Tiber beneath (the colour of gold, the sentimentalists say, the colour of mus-tard, the realists)" (James 1909). Goethe barely mentions it, nor do Lord Byron, Charles Dickens, or Mark Twain. The river where Romulus and Remus supposedly washed ashore attracted little attention from the travelers of the Grand Tour, more interested in seeking out monu-ments and works of art rather than reflect on the natural setting which gave birth to Roman culture. And yet it was there, alive and connected.

On 28 December 1870, just months after Italian nationalists breach the Aurelian Walls (establishing Rome as the nation's new capital), the Tiber river breached its banks and flooded the city to a level not seen since 1637. The nascent nation's capital was mortified by the em-barrassing inaugural performance, and flood-prevention measures, which had been discussed and debated since the late Republic, became urgent. Smart solutions such as bypass canals to mitigate extreme water levels were set aside in favor of the most destructive option: demolition of the fabric along the river and construction of the tall embankments walls, the *muraglioni*, which we see today.

Between 1880 and 1900 vast tracts of land on both sides of the Tiber were commandeered and cleared. The narrow streets of the former Jewish ghetto and the dense wall of buildings which had stood directly along the river, forming an occupied architectural edge, were all razed to be replaced by speculative modern structures. In fact, the creation of the Tiber embankment served both infrastructure and urban renewal, in the worst sense of the word, not unlike the cleansing efforts which would mar American cities and infuriate Jane Jacobs in the middle of the following century.

Rising forty feet from the lower riverside paths, these travertine walls effectively severed the city from its river. In her touchstone 2009 essay entitled *Rome's Uncertain Tiberscape*, Kay Bea Jones describes how "with street life, bridge crossing, and public activities now thriving fifteen meters above the Tiber's water level, which rises and falls with little effect, the relationship of modern Romans to their river was detached and would be changed forever" (Jones 2009). Since the completion of the embankment walls, Rome's riverfront has stood as a piece of obsolete and abandoned infrastructure, marginalized like the distant periphery despite its location in the heart of Rome. For many Romans and foreign *romaphiles* alike this neglect is unacceptable.

3. Tevereterno Onlus

Of all the initiatives to reactivate Rome's river, none have had such a tangible presence as Tevereterno, the creation of New York artist Kristin Jones. I first met Kristin in 2005 when she asked to meet me to talk about how the non-profit organization I had co-founded and was then serving as President, the American Institute for Roman Culture, might become her fiscal sponsor. Kristin had come to Rome in the 1980s with a Fulbright, and later returned as a Fellow at the American Academy where her project was focused on the potential of the Tiber riverfront as a site for artistic programming. Not the whole riverfront, but a particular section, between Ponte Sisto and Ponte Mazzini, which Kristin dubbed "Piazza Tevere", where the embankment walls run parallel to one another for a half a kilometer, cut perpendicularly by the two bridges to form a perfectly rectangular space. She observed that the space was like two New York blocks, four times as long as London's Tate Modern turbine hall, and the same size and proportions as Rome's largest ancient racetrack, the Circus Maximus.

Like most piazzas in Rome, there was water. Unlike typical Roman piazzas though, there was also vegetation, making it a rare example of green infrastructure in the heart of Rome (though Rome has more green space per capita than any other European capital, little of this is in the city center where most visitors concentrate). What was missing was the recognition as a public space and a reason to go there. In 2007, makeshift "street signs" appeared along with the first artistic programming and Piazza Tevere started to come to life.

Up to this point Tevereterno had been a vision, but in order to turn this vision into reality, an organization was needed. Kristin called on friends, old and new, in Rome's cultural community – Architects Carlo Gasparrini, Rosario Pavia and Luca Zevi – and, together, three Italian architects and one American artist, they formed the Associazione Tevereterno Onlus. The Italian term "Onlus" is short for non-profit organization with a social mission. With the help of other artists, composers and activists, Italian and American, Kristin began to plan and develop the first artistic programs to activate Piazza Tevere.

Kristin Jones has always been the main force behind Tevereterno, and the first projects were of her own creation. In 2005, with the aid of Capitoline Museums Director Claudio Parisi Presicce, who helped provide hundreds of images, she drew twelve *She Wolves* first on paper and then, using transparent plastic stencils, onto the embankment walls. She used a process of power-washing which would a decade later be used by William Kentridge. Later that year, on the night of the summer solstice, thousands of torches illuminated the river's edge (one for every year since the city's founding). An even greater number of people (estimated at close to 4.000) attended the event and heard the 100-member harmonic international choir directed by Roberto Laneri.

It would become a Tevereterno tradition to celebrate both the solstice and Rome's birthday on Piazza Tevere. In 2006, thirteen visual artists and composers were invited to propose site-specific works. A high-fidelity sound system and six high-resolution video projectors were used to activate the site with light, images and sounds. The following solstice, a line of floating flames snaked upon the Tiber's surface in a program entitled *Flussi Correnti* which brought a collaboration between Kristin Jones, architect Daniel K. Brown and a live, musical performance by the Roman ensemble Ars Ludi.

As Tevereterno's reputation grew, other creative individuals were drawn to Piazza Tevere, collaborating with the organization on projects of their own. Jenny Holzer projected massive written texts, a project entitled "For the Academy" in May 2007. In 2010 Robert Hammond (Co-Founder of New York's Friends of the High Line), with composer Lisa Bielawa produced *Chance Encounter*. Iconic red cafe chairs were purchased and scattered across the site, to be activated by passersby and documented in time-lapse photography.

The parallels between Piazza Tevere and the High Line were many: two examples of abandoned infrastructure in the heart of major cities, one (in New York) a success story of civic place-making, and the other still in the process of emerging. Even before Hammond's involvement, Tevereterno began to resonate globally, born of an international team in a city long-dubbed "caput mundi." In 2008 it brought Rome to New York's River To River Festival. In 2010 Tevereterno was present at the Architecture Biennale in Venice.

The international press loved it, but in Rome itself the project remained enigmatic. It seemed as if the potential of the Tiber could be seen better from afar. Or that the ephemeral, circumscribed interventions were too subtle for the city's administrators. Initiatives with am-

bitious titles such as "Progetto Millennium" were being launched, proposing new tourist hubs, airports, seaports, stadiums and a new metro
line. The Tiber, although recognized as crucial in the 2004 Master Plan,
was simply easy too (to) ignore. After all, it had been essentially forgotten since the embankment walls went up in the 1880s.

In a small way my own design work had touched on the Tiber over
the years, addressing difficult sites adjacent to the river such as the
abandoned Mira Lanza soap factory off Viale Marconi and the former
Papal Arsenale near Porta Portese. The Tiber lent itself to the application of a methodology I had developed in my teaching about sustainable urbanism. I had pinpointed seven interconnected themes and
insisted that any urban design intervention be accountable for addressing issues of water management, green space, urban fabric, energy use and conservation, waste reduction, mobility, and community
(Rankin, 2015). The Tiber is Rome's most visible water resource, and
even after the embankment walls it still poses a flood threat to the island and the river walkways and bikeways. It is also the most central
green infrastructure in Rome and provides a welcome respite from the
dense fabric of historic Rome and Trastevere. Today its role in hydro-
electric energy production is minimum, but the Tiber has a history of
floating mills which could return.

On and alongside the water, the river can serve Rome's mobility
needs as an alternative to its clogged and dangerous streets. Tiber
navigation, like its energy production once a major activity, is today
limited to a few tourist boats, but the potential is great. As a cyclist, I
often bike along the riverside bike trail (and was happy when the city
finally paved it in about 2010.) In collaboration with Engineer Antonio
Tamburrino I have been developing a proposal for new transit infrastructure, a major piece of which is tied to the Tiber. Finally, the Tiber
is Rome's drain, taking its wastewater and quite a lot else out to sea.
How can this be improved, reducing the river's pollution?

In short, the Tiber presents a series of environmental challenges
and opportunities, but until it is recognized as a significant place in
the city's cultural landscape, there is little political will to enact change.

It was for this reason that in early 2013 I accepted Kristin Jones' and the Tevereterno Onlus Board's invitation to serve as Director, to help usher in a new phase. Maybe a shot of public art would change the negative identity the river projected at present.

I had a dozen years of experience administering non-profits. I had created and run the Italian non-profit cultural association Scala Reale from 1996-2004, and then co-founded and managed the US 501c3 American Institute for Roman Culture until 2008. I knew that the first step to bringing order to the loose-knit organization was to draft and pass a strategic plan. The five-year plan approved by the board in October 2013 clarified the structure of Tevereterno which had previously been a personal artistic project of one artist, Kristin Jones. It set forth two independent but related organizations: the existing Italian organization and a planned "Friends of Tevereterno" which would be a US 501c3, run by an independent board, dedicated to raising funds for the Tiber projects and mission.

It established three divisions (Operations, Development and Projects), coordinated by the Director, who in turn would work under the governance and oversight of the Board. And of course this was accompanied by a five-year projected budget with allocations and expectations for these divisions. Predicted Revenues would start at about $80,000 in 2014 and reach almost half a million in 2018. The Strategic Plan contained a rudimentary campaign for crowdfunding and project sponsorship, as well as an outline for a necessary major outreach effort. With the plan approved, the organization started to grow; new board members, volunteers, and donors came on board and the authorities and press began to take notice.

4. William Kentridge

The administrative reorganization taking place behind the scenes, though essential to the health of the organization, was thoroughly eclipsed by the arrival in Rome of William Kentridge. The South

African virtuoso is one of the world's most important living artists, although in my ignorance I had never heard of him until Kristin introduced us and I attended his production of *Refuse the Hour* at the Teatro Argentina. I was immediately hooked, entranced by his rich interweaving of sound, text, image, of science, history, literature, and personal anecdote. *Refuse the Hour* reawakened the passion for theatre I had had just out of college, orbiting around the work of Robert Wilson and Philip Glass among others. At the same time Rome's MAXXI museum was showing Kentridge's installation entitled "The Refusal of Time", built around the same themes from the work of Peter Galison, a Harvard-based historian of science. I went back again and again.

Kristin had been following Kentridge's work for years and pressing him to consider a project for Piazza Tevere. In November 2012, while he was in Rome for *Refuse the Hour*, she set up a test projection of images and video onto the embankment walls in order to show Kentridge the possibilities. He watched from above, and then descended to the riverbanks below, observing the scale of the images (his own drawings from the recent performance).

After the last performance of *Refuse the Hour* there was a party in the spacious, art-filled home of a mutual friend off of Piazza Venezia. People who had been instrumental in Tevereterno over the years were in attendance, people like Andrea Canapa, Damiana Leoni and Pino Fortunato (who I learned held the position of Director, for which I was being recruited). Missing, because she was taking a rare leave of absence, was Diane Roehm who, after Kristin herself, was the single most active individual in the project, although she had no official role in the organization.

But none of the confusion of Tevereterno mattered; all eyes were on William Kentridge. When he spoke, it was his creative mind and his love of Rome that mattered, and his decision, after years of persistent cultivation on the part of Kristin, to embark on his first ever experience in free public art, here, on Piazza Tevere. "If not now, when?" he announced.

5. Triumphs and Laments

It was as if the floodgates had opened and the creative forces rushed on through. The proposed medium, selective cleaning of the river walls, had been tested and approved, but the exact subject had not yet been identified. Kentridge wasn't going to start drawing without assurance that permits and funding would be in place to make the project a reality, but ideas started to take form. He was interested in iconography from Rome's long and ongoing history, specifically images recognizable as victory or defeat, triumphs or laments. Under the direction of art historian Lila Yawn, professor at the nearby John Cabot University, a team was organized to collect images for Kentridge to draw from, and eventually a selection which he would draw in his studio. Two databases (one for triumphs and one for laments) were quickly merged into one when it became clear that every victory represented another's defeat, for every triumphal celebration someone else was mourning their losses.

Kentridge is remarkably humble for an artist of his stature. He listened with childlike fascination to explanations of images, to stories from Rome's history. He learned, he made connections, but as a visual artist, not a historian, he gravitated to the images themselves independent of the story they told. An emaciated horse from the base of Trajan's column, the Renault 4 with its hatch swung open to reveal the body of Aldo Moro, the war-worn prisoners carrying their treasures from the Arch of Titus, all were chosen for the emotions evoked, not for the specific message conveyed.

Parallel to the first iconographic research, another process was underway, the quest for signatures. Tevereterno Vice-President Valeria Sassanelli and I sent around documents, scheduled appointments, rescheduled appointments, met with officials, and patiently and persistently pushed to obtain the necessary permits. At each pass I filed away contact information in our growing database and added nodes to a map I called *Tiber Bureaucracy*. So many stakeholders played a role in Rome's river. Some thirteen were directly responsible, from the Lazio

Region to Roma Capital down to the Primo Municipio, AMA, ACEA and the Polizia Fluviale, but many others had an indirect interest in the river's health: international cultural institutes, embassies, environmental organizations, sporting clubs, and many, many others. The map became a sort of octopus.

And the process became what Kentridge would describe as an operatic drama: "One could do an interesting timeline of refusals and newspaper articles and phone calls [...] waiting for this politician to be thrown out or to resign and for a new one to come in" (Kentridge, 2016b). We met with Maria Costanza Pierdominici, 'Soprintendente per i Beni Architettonici e Paesaggistici per il Comune di Roma' who spoke positively of the project, and days later sent us a menacing letter critical of the project. Architect Federica Galloni, who first affirmed that she would never allow the project to take place, would in the end become one of its most ardent supporters and even write the dedication in the Ministry's publication about the project. We met with Raniero De Filippis of ARDIS who pledged his support, but days later he was arrested for alleged involvement in a corruption scandal. We spoke with the Minister of Cultural Heritage and the Performing Arts Massimo Bray who said he supported the project but had little power over the technicians working under him. We sat down with Ilaria Borletti Buitoni, then Undersecretary of the Ministry, and received her pledge of support. Actor Carlo Verdone met with us and agreed to become Tevereterno's *presidente onorario*. I brought U.S. Ambassador John Phillips and his wife Linda Douglass to Piazza Tevere where they participated in our annual 'Tevere Pulito' clean-up. Rome's MAXXI museum of contemporary art agreed to partner with Tevereterno, especially President Giovanni Melandri who is a great fan of Kentridge. The network of supporters mushroomed.

But at the same time there was a mixed reaction in the press, beginning with a headline in Rome's daily newspaper "Il Messaggero" which included the word 'graffiti'. The mistaken idea that a foreign artist would be invited to scrawl his graffiti on the walls of Rome's monuments (not at all what the project entailed) obviously aroused the rage of many Romans and it took a huge public relations effort on our part to explain that as an organization we were cleaning up the site, and the artistic medium was actually cleaning the walls. But the press, especially the art journal "Artribune", began to see the importance of the work and positive articles appeared worldwide.

In June 2014 Tevereterno organized an event at the MAXXI, an artists' workshop culminating in a projection and performance. Rome's art world was present in numbers, as were journalists, but with few exceptions the event was boycotted by all levels of public administration. Each time I spoke with Mayor Ignazio Marino, he said he supported the project, but he never made a proactive effort to bring it to fruition. When a meeting between Marino and Kentridge finally took place it was a fortuitous one, the artist on a boat, filming footage for a future documentary, the Mayor on his bike along the riverside path. It was thanks to Kristin Jones' quick thinking that the impromptu meeting even happened.

By mid-2015 the arduous permitting process was achieving its desired results and Kentridge began drawing without reserve. Now that "Triumphs and Laments" was moving forward it became urgent to raise the required funds, but the management of the project was problematic. The Artistic Director Kristin Jones, who was to report to me as Tevereterno Director in order to coordinate fundraising efforts, continued to act autonomously as she had always done. Kentridge's studio, rather than risking what must have seemed a disorganized collaboration with an inexperienced team, chose a professional outside producer with whom they had worked in the past. The project soon had three competing fundraising efforts running in parallel, only one of which brought funds to the organization that had launched the project years earlier and was working full-time to make it happen. As the deadline came closer, the strategic plan which the Tevereterno board had approved was boldly and bombastically disregarded, like the traffic laws on Rome's streets. Jones changed password access to the organization's website, and the whole communications and outreach plan came to a standstill just months from the anticipated initiation date of the selective cleaning work.

If it weren't for Kentridge's galleries taking on the responsibility for paying for the cleaning and the inaugural events, the project would have failed at this point. There was simply not enough money. Some compensation was also paid to certain Tevereterno board members but not to the administrative staff nor the development team who continued to work for free. However, the project was too exciting to be sidetracked by financial limitations.

Despite these obstacles, "Triumphs and Laments" moved forward to completion. Gianfranco Lucchini oversaw the technical production, specifically the transformation of the digital drawings emerging from Kentridge's studio into polycarbonate stencils. Starting in early March 2016, these were suspended against the embankment walls while workers in cherry pickers sprayed water against the stone surface, cleaning away the dirt. As the first stencils were removed, the figure of Mussolini on a horse emerged, his raised hand severed and floating ominously in a Roman salute just above the horse's tail, the whole thing riddled with what looked like shrapnel. Then Pasolini's body, Remus, the head of Cicero, and Minerva. The cleaning started in the middle and worked outwards until early April when all eighty or ninety figures (depending on how one counts them) were visible. Soon preparations would be underway for the inaugural events, the most ambitious theatrical spectacle William Kentridge had envisioned to date.

6. The Disappearing Frieze

From the moment the 500-meter long frieze was completed it began to decay back into nature. This is inherent in the ephemeral nature of the technique, and one of the reasons there was a sense of urgency to shine the spotlight on the work while it was fresh. Ironically the same authorities who had voiced opposition to the project early on, and who we had attempted to assuage with assurances that it was just a temporary work, now bemoaned the figure's impermanence. Once they realized that Rome had its own William Kentridge piece, they wanted it to be eternal, but Kentridge refused any suggestions of conserving it artificially. Rome, we pointed out, has a long tradition of ephemeral phenomena, from triumphal processions to Baroque processions to the Estate Romana festivals under cultural commissioner Renato Nicolini. The ephemeral actually leaves a more lasting impression on the viewer, Claudio Strinati pointed out, because the memories are left unadulterated by later transformations. "L'opera svanirà ma farà parte della storia e rimarrà nella coscienza della persone" (Strinati, 2014). What is certain is that anyone present 21-22 April, 2016 at the performances of Triumphs and Laments on Piazza Tevere will remember the experience for the rest of their lives.

That night, on a boat in the middle of the Tiber with good friends, in the company of William Kentridge who was also watching for the first time the unfolding of this performance, I felt that it had all been worth it. Thousands of people thronged the river's left bank and bridges to watch and experience the spectacle. It was evident that our mission, to reactivate the Tiber riverfront with site-specific art, had been achieved. The job was done, thanks to Tevereterno, its board and its founder Kristin Jones, thanks to William Kentridge, thanks to hundreds of supporters and volunteers, and even thanks to some administrators with a vision. The world had rediscovered Rome's river, and now things would change.

It would be nice if the story ended here, with the anticipation of improvements, of the physical transformation of the riverfront to make it more amenable to visitors, now that city officials had been shown what an important resource they had. An article in the New York Times by Elisabetta Povoledo, a few weeks after the inauguration, focused on the grassroots volunteer efforts of Tevereterno and others which indicated a change of current for Rome's river (Povoledo, 2016). It was clear that the next step would be to improve access, seating, lighting, to upgrade maintenance, in short to render Piazza Tevere a more presentable civic space on the international stage. Days before the inauguration, Tevereterno had been busy with almost a hundred volunteers cleaning the site, urging officials to find a reasonable solution for the homeless under the bridge. With the huge success of the event, I had no doubt that the playing field had changed.

Then a few weeks after the frieze was unveiled white tents began to be erected in front of it, tents which, if completed, would have effectively blocked its visibility. This should not have come as a surprise; for years agreements with other non-profit organizations had been in place to construct temporary structures along the riverfront, ostensibly for cultural activities, though in truth it seems that the organizations holding these concessions simply sublet them for a much greater fee than they paid to the city.

I had announced my resignation from Tevereterno at the completion of "Triumphs and Laments" and wasn't in a position to intervene. The organization's board remained silent, as did the authorities who had pleaded with Kentridge to make his work permanent. Only a group of private citizens spoke up, circulating a petition and staging protests, until the city suspended the construction of tents on Piazza Tevere.

But even so, Piazza Tevere fell back into a state of abandon. The homeless living under Ponte Mazzini returned, the weeds began to grow back, the stench, broken bottles and syringes again filled the stairs. In early July a young American student enrolled in a study abroad program at John Cabot University was found dead in the Tiber. The last people to see him alive were the denizens of Ponte Mazzini with whom he had been seen having an altercation, the same people who apparently still occupy the public space illegally today.

People came to see Kentridge's masterpiece but the dirty Tiber and its abandoned riverfront left an uncertain impression. When tagging showed up on the frieze in April 2016 the city acted to have it removed. But the tagging elsewhere on the site remained, although AMA was ready to clean it if the city gave the go-ahead. When the annual Tevere Pulito civic cleanup came around on Earth Day no one from Tevereterno or from the city government showed up.

Even Google recognizes Piazza Tevere as a place in its map data-base. Thousands of people have made the pilgrimage to the site to see Kentridge's biggest artwork. However, even after the huge international success of Triumphs and Laments, the city of Rome may not be ready to rethink its riverfront.

7. Conclusions

What could Piazza Tevere become with proper public investment, interventions, regulation and maintenance? "Triumphs and Laments" made its potential clear as a public space. It fills a void in Rome's rich offerings. The city has a plethora of *piazze* but they are, for the most part, hard-scaped urban spaces with a dearth of green space, little public seating, and no real sanctuary from ubiquitous motor vehicles. Piazza Tevere and the Tiber riverfront in general would provide an alternative public space for Rome, a linear green park where residents and guests could unwind from the intensity of urban life.

In lower Manhattan the transformation of the abandoned rail lines into the High Line brought about enormous change in the way that neighborhood is perceived and used. It also led to a huge increase in property value and tourist revenues. Similarly, Rome's forgotten infrastructure, its riverfront, could spawn an urban renaissance. The hard part has been done. Now is when – in a normal city – the administration would step in to provide the much needed upgrades and maintenance. Working with local associations, first and foremost with Tevereterno, it could fund competitions for public seating, lighting, and new ramps and elevators to make the site accessible. In place of the large-scale disorderly and banal tents which infest the riverfront each summer a competition could be launched for limited-scale, high-quality, temporary constructions, more Venice Biennale than country fair. The administration would treasure Rome's resources, especially its abandoned infrastructure, and work to instill new vitality in the city's many forgotten places.

Good architecture is like editing; we take what has come down to us over the ages, and analyze it critically, evaluating what works and what doesn't work. We use the existing as our raw material, whether it be vertical facades, stratified landscape, perspectival views or consolidated culture and commerce. The challenge for designers in a rich and complex urban context (none more so than Rome) is not to compete and to stand out. Nor should our objective be to embalm the past under glass, as if history has ended.

The early history of Piazza Tevere has shown that sometimes the most promising resources are right before our eyes, awaiting a fresh approach and a vision that artists serve to provide. The experience of "Triumphs and Laments" teaches us that good ideas are very often met with opposition or indifference, but that with perseverance they can reach fruition. Like so many initiatives in Rome, the creation of public art on Piazza Tevere was possible despite all of the obstacles the public administration placed in its way. Imagine what could result from a collaborative process involving progressive leaders and a motivated, innovative and international private sector.

References

James, H. (1909): "Italian Hours", in Project Gutenberg EBook, September 18th, 2016 (http://www.gutenberg.org/files/6354/6354-h/6354-h.htm)

Jones, K.B. (2009): "Rome's Uncertain Tiberscape": The Waters of Rome, 6, pp. 1-12.

Kentridge, W. (2016a): interview in https://www.enca.com/life/when-rome-see-kentridges-new-masterpiece, Agence France-Presse.

Kentridge, W. (2016b): interview in "William Kentridge, Triumphs and Laments, Todos Contentos Y Yo Tambien".

Lagunes, S./Margarita, M. (2004): Il Tevere e Roma; Storia di una simbiosi, Roma: Gangemi.

Mayne, T. (2011): Combinatory Urbanism, Culver City: Stray Dog Café.

Povoledo, E. (2016) "A Roman Legion of Volunteers Retakes the Tiber": New York Times, April 27th, (http://nyti.ms/1T1RR6l).

Rankin, T.G. (2015): Rome Works: An Architect Explores the World's Most Resilient City, Roma: Peruzzi.

Sennett, R. (1998): Raol Wallenberg Lecture November 30th (https://taubmancollege.umich.edu/pdfs/publications/map/wallenberg1998_richardsennett.pdf)

Strinati, C. (2014) "Grande idea", interview with Laura Larcan, Graffiti sul Tevere: Il Messaggero, January 9th.

2. MULTIPLE CULTURES FOR URBAN GOVERNANCE

BUILT HERITAGE AND MULTIPLE IDENTITIES IN MUMBAI
MATERIAL CULTURE AND CONSERVATION PRACTICES

Clarissa Pelino

1. Introduction: material culture and political economy

As cities of the world are faced with problems raised by increasing urbanization and globalization trends, arguably the most basic and inescapable issue they are confronted with is the fact that their aspirations to grow, and mold themselves elastically to rapid changes, clash inevitably and evidently with their physicality. Economic and social relations are constantly changing, but the architectural skeleton of our urban landscapes, made out of steel, stone, and concrete cannot respond as quickly.

In this scenario of tensions between weight and lightness, materiality and fluidity, where additionally land becomes increasingly scarce and density grows, logics of demolition and reconstruction that try to accommodate urban change have to deal with the desire, on the part of civil society or of politicians and city-branders, to preserve a certain "cityness". However, actors that live, use, and plan the city have different and often diverging ideas, interests, imageries of what the city looks or should look like, and of what use should be made of its built environment; all cities virtually exist, in people's cognitive landscapes, in millions of different forms, each slightly or completely different from the others, each representing a different identity and a specific type of "cityness". This makes it practically impossible, when it comes to urban change, to find consensus about which "cityness" one wants to preserve, and thus which pieces of the urban fabric should stay, and which ones should go.

Mumbai, more than other cities, is dealing with problems of extremely high land prices and scarcity of land. At the same time, its long history makes it a palimpsest of different political regimes, economic ways of production, and architectural styles. With its complex and archipelagic cartography of actors, in Mumbai even more than elsewhere lives a multitude of diverging images of "cityness", with different types of attachment to the urban fabric.

In its processes of urban change, different types of buildings have lived different stories, and I would like to point at the possible discriminating factors that result into varying degrees of conservation, demolition, or adaptive re-use. While the architectural and historic 'value' of the buildings – very frequent in the Indian legislation as a criterion – could be a factor, it remains a subjective matter, and I don't think it can appropriately explain the differences: being extremely subjective and volatile, depending even on fashion, culture, etc., it can be a tool, not a real variable, to discriminate conservable buildings from the ones that do not deserve preservation.

This chapter represents an effort to incorporate elements of material culture studies within a political economic analytical framework: in a same context of land regulations, traditions of conservation, and raising land values I will try to give some importance to the physical properties of buildings and to their meaning, which inevitably changes for different structures, uses, and owners. Ultimately, this chapter will try to look at the paths that different buildings in Mumbai have followed, and ask the questions: what do buildings mean, and for whom? And, could this be a relevant factor?

Starting from a material culture assumption of interaction between built form and social phenomena (Gieryn, 2002), I argue that (i) buildings and their materiality have a meaning for people, and this meaning is an important element in explaining their conservation or redevelopment trajectories, and (ii) in Mumbai, where conservation practices are decentralized, the value that the owners of the structures attribute to them, the relation they have to their physical existence matters sometimes more than the government's efforts in preserving certain memories and identities over others. I will draw examples from the Art Deco buildings in South Mumbai, especially the movie theaters, and from the industrial cotton mills of Girangaon.

2. Buildings, identity, and memory

Heritage preservation as a practice is strongly linked to the "character" that built structures help to preserve. The Indian *Handbook of Conservation of Heritage Buildings*, published in 2013, states as a criterion for the conservation of landscapes and structures the fact that they should "provide character and distinctive identity to cities". This confirms the assumption that buildings are often conserved, or not, based on whether they are considered to be a component of the city's identity. However, following the material culture assumption that there is an interaction between built forms and social phenomena (Gieryn, 2002), different buildings, with their different architectural elements and historical pasts, give different materialities to the city, and trigger different types of "memory" in the viewers. Let's look at the Art Deco buildings and at the industrial structures more closely as examples.

Mumbai's Art Deco heritage is one of the richest in the world, second only to Miami's. Designed by Indian as well as European architects during the 30s and 40s, it is comprised of residential, administrative, and commercial facilities, all located in South Mumbai. In the 1920s, 1930s, and 1940s the Art Deco style spoke a narrative of modernity, and its development in Mumbai is representative of the post-war growth of a local bourgeoisie, with aspirations for the city to be modern, sophisticated, and cosmopolitan. Art historian Michael Windover understands Art Deco as a style which conveys a universal artistic and architectural language of mobility, where shapes such as the streamline served as visual and physical representations of the new modern aesthetics and ways of life. In particular, he argues that Bombay Deco is making a statement of "cosmopolitanism", which includes in its meaning the question of mobility as well as the "willingness to borrow from multiple sources", while remaining tied to an "elite class association, even in more 'democratic' forums, such as movie theaters" (Windover, 2012: 174). This language is arguably very much embedded in Art Deco's visual style, in the graphicness and uniqueness of its forms: its lines and shapes speak to us, like an alphabet, and say "modern".

While Art Deco buildings convey ideas of a modern, bourgeois urbanity, the built industrial landscape of Mumbai speaks a very different language. Its structures, namely the mills and the residential *chawls*, bring back memories of an industrial past that powerful actors in Mumbai have been recently overcoming in their effort to make the city more global, cosmopolitan, and attractive to local and international investment (Chatterjee 2013, Nainan 2008). The mills and the *chawls* convey the imagery of a manufacturing-based society, that is being substituted in Mumbai by a "post-industrial" economic model, materially concretized in tall office towers, commercial centers, and gated communities. The industrial landscape, Chatterjee (2013) argues, was "considered to be the birth place of the working class and its culture in the city": now that the image of the city is changing, the working class is being displaced towards the outskirts, while the city-center is being re-crafted through operations of demolition and reconstruction, aimed at making it speak a language of globalization, service-economy, and commerce.

The Art Deco buildings of Mumbai, with very few exceptions, are still present as of today in their original form, while the vast majority of the mills have been redeveloped throughout the 1990s and 2000s. If we stand by the material culture assumption that architectural forms do have a social and cultural meaning, we could intuitively say that the Art Deco buildings are surviving redevelopment because, contrarily to industrial structures, they speak a language – no matter how outdated in the 2010s – that fits into today's most powerful idea of "cityness": the one being propelled by public institutions and bourgeois actors.

However Mumbai's case is surprising: as we will see in the following section, the Art Deco structures do not enjoy much greater attention from the government in terms of conservation than the mills do.
It can be argued, instead, that in Mumbai the government is not fully
responsible for this discrimination, because in fact it does not actively
engage in preservation practices in the city.

3. The State and preservation: a decentralized approach

The previous section maintains that different materialities in the built
environment evoke different imageries of the city, and thus imply different potentials for preservation. In her paper "Mumbai's Quite Histories" Nakamura argues that the logic of heritage preservation "is by
its very nature exclusionary; as a form of enclosure it valorizes some
material pasts and futures over others" (2014: 272). Although this fits
in with the above explored idea of a connection between materiality,
identity, and memory, in some ways such a statement logically leads us
to imagine the actor in charge of preservation practices to be unitary,
and to set up and enforce regulations in a way that leads to the conservation of a certain type of memory over others, in an effort to give
a consciously selected historical and material character to the city. If
we imagine preservation as the practice of one single agent, we would
by consequence imagine this agent to be the government, the one in
charge of the regulatory system. In the case of Mumbai, though, is this
true? Do the government's preservation efforts really account for the
fate of material structures in the city?

India has a long and important tradition in heritage preservation:
in 1861 the Archeological Survey of India (ASI) was established to "ini-
tiate legal provision to protect the historical structures all over India"[1];
the Indian National Trust for Art and Cultural Heritage (INTACH) was

---

1 "Handbook of Conservation of Heritage Buildings", 2013, published by the Directorate General, Central Public Works Department, p. 3.

founded in 1984 to promote heritage preservation through the Country at large. The INTACH developed a Listing of Heritage Buildings, based on a grading of buildings (Grade I, II, III) with different levels of conservation, mainly based along the lines of geographical and social importance and identity ("national" for Grade I, "regional" or "local" for Grade II, and finally related to the townscape, or to the lifestyle of a particular community, for Grade III).

Despite this important framework, the institutions in charge of enforcing preservation are not particularly powerful. In Mumbai, the provisions put forward by the Mumbai Heritage Conservation Committee (MHCC, created in 1990) are often ignored by planning agencies, as it was the case with the publishing of the 2014-2034 Development Plan for Greater Mumbai[2], which ignored over 70 per cent of the heritage structures in the city[3], giving rise to a huge controversy amongst conservation architects and planners.

Additionally, it should be noted that the government does not propose itself (not even nominally) as a centralized and enforcing actor for preservation practices: the clause 8.2 of the *Conservation of Heritage Sites Including Heritage Buildings, Heritage Precincts and Natural Feature Areas* states that "it shall be the duty of the owners of heritage buildings and buildings in heritage precincts or in heritage streets to carry out regular repairs and maintenance of the buildings" (p. 130): the state thus decentralizes conservation practices, shifting the responsibility for the latter to the buildings' owners. However, it does not provide the owners with any particular incentives to engage in these practices, which is another point that the MHCC reproached to the 2014-2034 Development Plan[4]. As a result, many listed heritage buildings are now endangered. The example of the residential buildings of Marine Drive is blatant: falling under the Rent Control Act of 1947, the tenants living

---

2 "Government ignored heritage panel's advice for conservation incentives", The Indian Express, April 2nd, 2015.
3 "Treat Heritage as an Asset, not Liability", The Indian Express, April 23, 2015.
4 Ibid.

there pay rents that are frozen to 1940 levels, in an extremely expensive area. This creates a huge disincentive for the owners to re-modernize the structures, as doing so would involve very high expenditures with no returns.

4. Use value, exchange value, and individual practices of preservation

While the vast majority of Mumbai's industrial fabric has undergone redevelopment, the Art Deco structures largely remain standing, but that the state is not a strong enough agent in the city's preservation practices to fully account for this discrimination. We will see in this section that political economic factors of market trends and land regulations are in some cases not exhaustive variables to explain the phenomenon: the focus will shift to individual owners and users of the buildings, who, as I am arguing, offer a better understanding of the different trajectories of built heritage structures in Mumbai.

In this section, specifically, elements of material culture will intermingle with political economic questions and mechanisms. I will use Marx's distinction between *use value* and *exchange value* as a conceptual starting point in order to understand the different relationships that link buildings to their owners and users, and the different meanings that buildings can have for individual actors. This will allow us to understand the preservation of buildings in Mumbai through a perspective that takes into account the attachment of the owners to their meanings and physical structures: the land regulatory frameworks and market trends that are typical of a political economic perspective can maybe explain the redevelopment of the mills, but do not suffice in the case of the Art Deco theatres. This is because the actors' relationships to the buildings are fundamentally, essentially different.

In the first chapter of *The Capital* Marx writes of use value as "an aspect of the commodity [which] coincides with the physical palpable existence of the commodity"; he goes on: "the utility of a thing makes it a use value. But this utility is not a thing of air. Being limited to the physical properties of the commodity, it has no existence apart from that commodity" (p. 17). On the other hand the concept of exchange value, which is concerned with the quantitative properties (essentially, money) of commodities, makes different commodities with the same exchange value indifferent between themselves. To put it – simplistically – in practical terms, if I consider a coat for its use value, trading it for a diamond would not make sense; but if I consider the coat's exchange value, trading it for a diamond would be a very convenient deal.

Now leaving Marx aside, and his well-known critique of capitalism that follows, let's try to apply this concept to our case. Use value is concerned with the palpability and materiality of an object, while exchange value takes into consideration the amount of profit that the object will be able to provide, either through further trade, or because it represents an asset for capital transformation. The owners and users of the buildings we are taking into consideration attribute a different type of value to the different structures, and this difference represents a way of understanding the preservation trajectories that they followed.

Let's take the example of the Art Deco movie theatres, which are for the most part still family-run: the owners of these buildings, who are – as provided for by the "Conservation of Heritage Sites Including Heritage Buildings, Heritage Precincts and Natural Feature Areas" – the ones in charge of their preservation, seem to be enormously attached to the structures and to their physical materiality, despite adverse regulation, taxation, and fierce competition from multiplexes not allowing them to make profit.

In terms of regulations, the Maharashtra Cinema (Regulation) Rules of 1966 states in its clause 125 that "no cinema premises shall be used for any purpose other than the exhibition of cinematograph films (musical and dance performances, display of electronic and video transmitted images and conference facilities)". This means that the owners, who are attached to the structures and for the most part reluctant to sell out to multiplexes, cannot truly diversify their business activities, making it really hard for single-screen theaters to survive, as the adaptive re-use of the structures is not an option.

Additionally, the Bombay Rent Control Act of 1947, which provided for a rent-freeze to 1940-levels of privately owned structures and apartments, has kept the owners' rental possibilities very limited[5]. In terms of taxation, while the multiplexes have been treated with indulgence since their first appearance, the old single-screens find it basically impossible to make profit. The Entertainment tax provides for 45 per cent of the profit on each ticket in single-screens to be given to the State of Maharashtra, while the rest is split between the theatre and the producer/distributor.

To give a specific example, Nazir Hoosein, owner of the Liberty Cinema and son of the original owner Habib Hoosein, has maintained the theatre in its original Art Deco form, but is experiencing great difficulties in running the structure: while it takes 9 lakhs (about 14,000 USD) per year to run, high taxation on the movie tickets makes revenues extremely low (27 rupees per ticket – about 40c USD). The high costs of film purchases, together with an electricity bill of 400,000 rupees (about 6000 USD) per year for only three screenings a month, is making it extremely difficult for the theatre to keep the shows going, so Hoosein is renting it out for music and theatre events. He is also renting locales in one wing of the building for office use, but since the structure falls under the Bombay Rent Control Act of 1947, the charges cannot go higher than 1 rupee (about 1c USD) per square foot, in an area where land is extremely expensive[6].

However, Hoosein has so far continued taking care of the structure as much as possible, and visibly appreciates its architectural and design qualities. He says: "Wood has been used extensively in the cinema, and consists of a blend of Canadian cedar and Burma teak. The carpeted foyer is another unique feature. The actual heavy-duty main-

---

5 In 2015 the State decided to exclude properties of over 500 square feet for residential, and of over 800 square feet for commercial purposes, from the Act.

6 "The math doesn't add up for Mumbai's Art Deco cinemas", Livemint, May 19th 2009.

tenance at the hall is done almost daily. The carpets and the woodwork go through daily cleaning".[7]

The Liberty is not an exception: other theaters, such as the Regal, are following similar trajectories, their structures being saved and preserved by the perseverance and attachment of the owners. The owners see in these buildings something unique whose value would be lost if the land – although very expensive – were to be sold for multiplex redevelopment, as it happened to the Metro Theater. Additionally, these structures embody for them a tradition of movie-going and a collective past for the community of South Mumbai, representing a space of social proximity and gathering (Mabbott, Athique and Hill, 2007: 108-118). This type of value is a use value: though the buildings do not produce much profit (actually, they incur into losses), their value would not exist outside of their physical existence, and therefore transforming them into something else would not make sense.

A completely different case is that of the Girangaon Mills. First of all, factories as buildings are intrinsically different from movie theaters. Not only have their imagery – that of an industrial society – been (arguably wrongly) associated with filth, poverty, and danger. But as structures, they essentially represent tools for capital transformation: they are understood as the machines that generate value, not the value itself; they do not have a public, but rather they host the economic productivity of the city. The structures may be not so valuable for themselves, or for the qualitative use that was made of them, as it is the case for the movie theatres; instead, their owners saw their value in quantitative terms, in terms of exchange value, which made the physical structures fairly interchangeable with other, new ones that would generate more profit. Thus, in a framework where preservation practices are decentralized, a smaller potential for conservation.

In terms of regulations, while before 1991 the cotton textile mills were protected as the economic engine of the city, the new Develop-

---

7 "Mumbai's Art Deco heritage a nod to a history of style", The National, March 29th, 2013.

ment Control Regulations of 1991, and in particular the clause 58, allowed for "sick mills" to be redeveloped. In case of demolition of the structure, the one-third rule applied: 33 per cent of the land had to go to the BMC (Brianmumbai Municipal Corporation) for the creation of public spaces and amenities; 27 per cent was to be given to the MHADA (Maharashtra Housing and Area Development Authority) for public housing, and finally 40 per cent could be used by the owner for the development of commercial or residential buildings.

The one-third rule, with slightly different percentages, also applied to "lands of cotton textile mills for purpose of modernization" (but only 33 per cent to the owner), and to land of cotton mills that were being relocated outside the city-center (with only 30 per cent for private redevelopment). This made it more convenient for all mill owners (and 33 out of 48 mills were privately owned) to let the structures fall sick rather than to re-modernize them, especially after the textile industry had been de-licensed by Congress in 1991. Additionally, in 2001 the DCR 58 was amended, providing that the one-third rule only applied to the vacant land of the plot (that which was not occupied by the mill's structure).

This, of course, created incentives for the owners to sell the mill land for redevelopment: by the 90s, the value that the owners would get from the land as an asset to be transformed was far higher than the value that the textile production was able to give them. Without the owners' attachment to the materiality of the buildings, market factors and legislations remain the only solid variables for the understanding of redevelopment. However, an enquiry on the type of relationship that the owner has to the physicality of the structures is necessary, prior to excluding material culture factors from the equation. People who are attached to buildings and attribute to them what I defined in this chapter as a use value will go past economic rationality and complicate the scenario of conservation practices, as even a negative balance sheet will not be enough big an incentive to push them to sell.

5. Conclusions

This chapter represents an effort – though far from being exhaustive – to combine material culture studies with a political economic analysis to further the understanding of built heritage preservation in Mumbai. The case of Mumbai is interesting because the government, though equipped with a solid institutional and regulatory framework for conservation, actually does not play an active role in enforcing and carrying out preservation projects; additionally, it decentralizes the responsibility for preservation to the individual owners of the structures, without providing them with the necessary incentives. In this respect, the idea that the state's practices of discretionary conservation can fully explain buildings' trajectories is to be excluded.

When it comes to individual practices, it becomes useful to employ Marx's distinction between use and exchange value, in order to look at what type of meaning different buildings have for their owners and for those in charge of their preservation or redevelopment. While regulations, taxation, economic trends and incentives are very important factors accounting for land use practices in a city as dense as Mumbai, they are not always sufficient, and elements of interaction between the buildings and the owners should also be taken into account for a more comprehensive framework of understanding.

References

Chatterjee, D.(2013); "Gentrification in the mill land areas of Mumbai City: A case study", paper presented at the International RC 21 Conference, Berlin, August 29th-31st.

Crinson, M. (2005, ed.): Urban Memory: History and Amnesia in the Modern City, London: Routledge.

Gieryn, T.F. (2000): "A Space for Place in Sociology", Annual Review of Sociology, 26, pp. 463-496.

Gieryn, T.F. (2002): "What Buildings Do", in Theory and Society: 31/1, pp. 35-74.

Gupta, N. (2001): "Of Giants and Jewelers: The Monumental and The Miniature in India's Historic Landscapes": Thesis Eleven 105/1, pp. 35-43.

Mabbott, A.A./Hill, D. (2007): "Multiplex Cinemas and Urban Redevelopment in India": Media International Australia, 124, pp. 108-118.

Marx, K., (2013): "Capital: A Critical Analysis of Capitalist Production", London: Wordsworth Editions.

Naiman, N., (2008): "Building Boomers and Fragmentation of Space in Mumbai", Economic and Political Weekly: 43/21, pp. 29-34.

Narain Lambah, A. (2012): "Mumbai: Historic Preservation by Citizens", in Anheier, H./Raj Isar, Y. (eds.): Cities, Cultural Policy and Governance, Newbury Park CA: Sage, pp. 251-256.

Windover, M. (2012): "Art Deco: A Mode of Mobility", Montréal: Presse de l'Université de Québec.

Legal documents

"Development Control Regulations" of 1991, Municipal Corporation of Greater Mumbai.

"Conservation of Heritage Sites Including Heritage Buildings, Heritage Precincts and Natural Feature Areas", Town & Country Planning Organization, Ministry of Urban Development, Government of India.

"Bombay Rents, Hotel, and Lodging House Rates Control Act", 1947.

"Maharashtra Cinemas (Regulation) Act", 1953.

Press

"Government ignored heritage panel's advice for conservation incentives", The Indian Express, April 2, 2015.

"Treat Heritage as an Asset, not Liability", The Indian Express, April 23, 2015.

"The math doesn't add up for Mumbai's Art Deco cinemas", Livemint,
    May 19th 2009.
"Mumbai's Art Deco heritage a nod to a history of style", The National,
    March 29th, 2013

Other

"Handbook of Conservation of Heritage Buildings", Directorate General, Central Public Works Department, July 2013

THE IMMIGRATION ISSUE IN INTERNATIONAL DEBATE ON URBAN SOCIETIES' CHANGES

Domenica Moscato

1. Foreword

The immigration issue and its settlement are very complex and controversial. The impact it generates on societies is significant and extends to all levels, from the national to the local, as well as on various fields such as the labour market, social welfare, education, culture and housing. International debate on the topic has augmented over the last decade as increased flows of immigration have influenced the daily lifestyles of individuals and their traditional models of reference, above all with regard to work and family.

However, the creation of social and cultural pluralism in societies, and Western societies more specifically, is part of a broader transformation affecting demographic and economic factors connected to globalization and the reconversion of post-industrial contexts. According to the paper "World Population Prospects: The 2017 Revision" published by the UN Department of Economic and Social Affairs (2017), there continues to be a significant migration phenomenon among the different regions of the world, particularly from low-income Countries towards more industrialized, highly developed Nations. Around 2.2 million people per year migrated in the period from 2010 to 2015, reflecting global economic disparity and highlighting two important factors, typical of industrial societies: high productivity and ageing

populations with decreasing birth rates. These types of Countries continue to generate better employment prospects, thereby becoming pull
factor Countries that attract populations from areas still in a phase
of development or political restructuring; people from such areas mi-
grate by covering the so-called 'ddd jobs' (dirty, dangerous, demean-
ing) that are low-skill in order to improve their living conditions. The
interrelationship between the uneven distribution of world income
between countries and the demographic crisis of the most advanced
Countries thus becomes fundamental in the comprehension and overall reading of the phenomenon of migration.

It can be said, therefore, that the role of migration is to rebalance
the relationship between the demographic and economic deficit in the
world, which presents an opportunity for double development: on the
one hand, it can contribute to reducing the minimal growth and demographic stagnation of rich Countries; on the other hand, it can also
improve the dynamics of development for densely-populated territories, many of which are in Countries where minimum welfare services
are not guaranteed. However, the link between the two sides of the
relationship must be regulated by effective policies that guarantee
benefits for both newcomers and host societies.

2. Integration as a key process

Since 2009, and in coherence with all European principles and traditions, the European Union has been trying to fill the migration gap
between EU Member Countries through a common immigration policy framework. Immigration decisions are shared among all member
States and European institutions, but better management of the issue
is needed for high-quality socioeconomic development. In the communication "A Common Immigration Policy for Europe" from the European Commission to the European Parliament, the European Council,
and the Committee of the Regions (2008), the vital role of immigration
is highlighted as a key factor for the labour market, the welfare state

and aging populations. Furthermore, the potential of immigration from the social integration point of view is recognized for its benefits in terms of cultural diversity. It allows the creation of an open-minded environment respectful of newcomers' needs, meanwhile the approach to integration is intended to be "a dynamic, two-way process of mutual accommodation by all immigrants and residents of Member States" according to the definition adopted by the European Union[1].

Integration is nothing more than a deepening of immigrants' settlement process that likewise involves the host society: according to Rinus Penninx (2014:16) "integration is the process of becoming an accepted part of society," a very basic definition that assumes there is a relationship in which the receiving society's role is more powerful than that of the newcomers due to the stronger sense of cohesion and belonging of residents. As stated by Penninx (ibid:16), the integration process works within three different spheres:

- The Legal and Political sphere refers to the legal status of immigrants and how their residency permits affect citizenship;
- The Socioeconomic dimension relates to the level of immigrants' engagement in sectors like the labour market, health services, education and housing;
- The Cultural and Religious dimension is the most difficult level to reach because it is a fine line between adaptation and acceptance of newcomers.

In the analysis of European immigration flows, there is no systematic approach to settlement. Usually, at the beginning of the flows, immigrants tend to arrive in metropolitan cities due to the large-scale job opportunities. However, the environment in which the integration process is best performed is the local dimension (neighbourhood or village), where the small scale allows newcomers to access basic services

---

1 "Glossary of the Directorate-General Migration and Home Affair of the European Commission", 2011 (https://ec.europa.eu/home-affairs/content/integration_en).

and offers the possibility to extend community networks with a higher impact on their sense of belonging. Thus, the local spatial dimension becomes the playing field on which close relations are triggered, as well as where relationships with institutions and the community are manifested as a "low social complexity" (Balbo et al. 2015: 10) that reflect a numerically limited system of stakeholders. In short, when foreign people arrive in a new place they immediately search for a source of income and a secure place to stay, in addition to connections with different people in order to satisfy their other necessities.

Everyday life in a small-scale environment inevitably entails encounters with difference and thereby requires individuals to find an appropriate way to coexist and fulfil social integration. Daily contact or spatial proximity, however, do not necessarily have consistent results; they could lead to mutual understanding, tolerance and inclusion, or to the opposite with racism, mistrust, conflict and stigmatization.

Focusing on everyday encounters and interactions in a local context brings to light the discourse of culture, the hybridization of differences, and how people can live together in culturally pluralistic societies due to the various nationalities newcomers have.

3. The role of the arts and culture for the integration process

In everyday life, immigrants' presence often produces a negative impact on the hosting community due to the fact that the diversity of newcomers is frequently associated with a threat to the local identity. A national identity is expressed through traditions, symbols, ceremonies, a shared history, and everything belonging to intangible cultural heritage, which can have an exclusionary effect on newcomers since they are unfamiliar with these aspects of the host Country.

While international political discourse focuses on disseminating a negative image of immigration with the need to defend the identity of nations welcoming immigrants, scientific literature seeks to promote the concept that culture plays a key role not only on the economic scene, but also with regard to social inclusion in cities with high immigration rates and diversity.

Since identity is closely connected to the field of culture, intercultural dialogue is the best way to create social cohesion and integration. In terms of definition, the European Commission affirms that "Intercultural dialogue is, essentially, the exchange of views and opinions between different cultures"[2]. It diverges from multiculturalism since its objective is to create a common understanding between citizens rather than a multicultural vision of separate identities that coexist. In daily life, interculturality represents a modification in behaviours and routines: for example, within the issue of minority group organisations, the intercultural view considers immigrants/newcomers as agents of integration, highlighting the importance of their role in societal changes and of their engagement in social life. Intercultural dialogue thus implies that individual views are secondary to collective voices and perspectives, and participation is the key factor for building up an even environment where immigrants and host citizens are involved in the same way.

If culture is the most important communication medium, artists play a central role in helping refugees in the integration process and exposing all people to diversity. Art in general allows the exploration of conflicts that could emerge due to the presence of immigrants whose culture may clash with that of the host community, and it offers tools and approaches for intervention and integration in communities.

In a refugee context, there are two successful factors that help migrants to become an essential part of the community – participation and empowerment – both of which contribute to the sense of belonging and the integration process. Both concepts are connected; participation encourages people to share opinions and express themselves as a preparatory step leading to empowerment, interpreted as "the

2 "European Commission", 2018 (https://ec.europa.eu/culture/policy/strategic-frame work/intercultural-dialogue_en)

process of becoming stronger and more confident, especially in controlling one's life and claiming one's rights" (Oxford Dictionary: 2018).

In conclusion, cultural projects and institutions should offer migrants and refugees suitable means of becoming more confident, organizing themselves, and removing obstacles to protect their civil rights and conditions for their participation in society.

4. Which successful framework in cultural projects?

The complexity of the immigration issue is due to the multi-dimensional aspects of migration requiring different regulations and policies that must be integrated. Firstly, immigration's policies play out on two levels:

- the national level that usually concerns security, citizenship rules and modes of entry and has an immediate effect on the immigration flows through means such as restrictive regulations that can lead to a decrease in entrances;
- the local level, which is considered the scene of integration because it deals directly with regulations related to social and economic settlement and more generally with the connection between the host community and immigrants.

Cultural strategies and projects follow the same approach as local and national policies in that projects are included within a national framework that strengthens identity as a collective feeling and promotes local actions, facilitating growth in the relationship between immigrants and locals and highlighting their connections with shared places.

In the last decade, following the substantial increase in migratory flows, the European Commission has placed immigration policies at the centre of its priorities. Additionally, the priority of fostering refugee integration has arisen in the cultural sector, which has launched a special call for proposals under the Creative Europe Programme[3] in order to fund cultural and audiovisual projects with the goal of enhancing intercultural dialogue and mutual understanding. Among 274 application proposals submitted in April 2016, twelve projects were approved, involving a partnership of 62 organisations in twenty European Countries with a budget of € 2.35 million. Such long-term and hefty financial investment has put into relief the need to assess activities as there is a lack of project evaluation in terms of qualitative indicators.

In a report[4] published in March 2017 by experts from the 2015-2018 Work Plan for Culture, the importance of evaluation of cultural projects is stressed so that policies and best practices in refugee and migratory contexts can be shared. The report affirms that there are a few criteria to successfully evaluate activities, and the majority of cultural projects rely on numerical outputs, such as the audience reached to evaluate success.

The critical issue to be evaluated is the weakness in recognizing the impact of intercultural dialogue on communities through the arts, although there is greater policy awareness of its effectiveness for a more inclusive and democratic society. In order to ensure success in cultural projects, experts identified the different tools listed below:

- *Partnership*
  It is important at any level that cultural projects include the participation of both institutions and civil society. A key element to develop more inclusive projects is that the partnership should be composed of public authorities and private stakeholders. Non-governmental organisations (NGOs) could be important partners because they usually have a high impact on public opinion due to their skills in campaigning and spreading awareness of issues.

---

3 "Creative Europe is the European Commission's framework programme for support to the culture and audiovisual sectors", 2018, (https://ec.europa.eu/programmes/creative-europe/about_en)
4 "How culture and the arts can promote intercultual dialogue in the context of the migratory and refugee crisis", 2017, Brussels, Publications Office of European Union.

- *Engagement of refugees/migrants*
  Activities should open up dialogue between migrants and nationals. A participatory process consisting of the presence of newcomers and experts together is the key to successful projects.
- *Training as a cross-cultural tool*
  Training as well as mobility in projects are important for acquiring specific or transversal skills such as organisational and communication skills, teamwork, etc. Training should also include support for migrants' languages and be informative about the migrants' cultures.
- *Sustainability*
  Guaranteeing sustainable projects is the general challenge of private organizations because financial resources are unstable and often depend on public funding or management systems that are sporadic rather than carried out within a long-term strategy. Sustainability could be achieved through a quality network where there is the possibility to exchange skills, an efficient dissemination of the activity results, and a strong rate of co-ownership among stakeholders and beneficiaries. Sustainability should include replicability and transferability: the former refers to the possibility of replicating the same initiative in another place, while the latter takes advantage of methodologies and processes and tries to implement them in future projects.

5. The urban spaces of difference

Discourses on immigrants' settlement causes necessary reflection on processes of territorialization, considering urban space as a field in which different practices and representations due to difference are generated. Urban space plays a key role in the relationship among different social actors, and it should be considered not only as "a container but a mediator" (Cancellieri et al. 2012: 65). Focusing on the importance of public space requires consideration for the new global dynamics of cities, which experience heterogeneity in density and population that increase their susceptibility to social conflicts.

A common element in the political, academic and public debate when it comes to urban transformations that have taken place in European post-industrial societies is the connection between immigration and social stigmatization: there is a shared opinion confirming the significant difference between the city centre and its outskirts, where immigrants tend to remain because of low accommodation costs. The gap that separates the cohesive city centre and suburban areas, marked by economic and social exclusion, justifies the spatial planning policy on urban redevelopment realised in big cities. The nucleus of cities represents a pull factor by offering a high labour market that attracts both resident workers and external city users, whereas suburban areas live in a permanent emergency situation in which the less well-off face lack of opportunity and space for social encounters. Very often immigrants' presence is linked to security issues, and policies that negatively influence public opinion intensify social conflicts that strain multi-ethnic coexistence. It is undeniable that immigrants have changed urban spatial processes by presenting a new element in public space, but scientific reflection requires a more objective analysis that differs from the securitarian approaches often implemented by urban policies.

When dealing with the issue of immigration, there is no definite result. Spatial proximity can produce two different effects: on the one hand, the presence of people from various geographical origins creates a multicultural environment that can be a stimulus for increasing the subjects' empowerment, both for residents and immigrants; on the other hand, the presence of diversity inside the same public space can turn into hypervisibility and give rise to exclusion. As quoted by Cancellieri, immigrants' settlement in a public space can produce "both esteem and stigma" (ibid: 68), the former referring to an improvement in the immigrants' ability to adapt, the latter to the genesis of social exclusion. Since policies take action based on the analysis of social relationships inside public spaces, it would be advisable to approach the issue of the 'visibility' of diversity with great caution and objectivity precisely because it can generate social recognition as well as the opposite, control and conflict.

The challenge of contemporary cities is to find solutions to the social complexity of international migration. The liveability of public space depends on several factors related to access, design, comfort, maintenance and sociability. In a place where diversity of gender, ethnicity and culture coexist, these differences are reflected in the use of space.

With regard to immigrants' settlement process, it is natural that social needs intertwine with those of other social actors, and a number of authors from the scientific community have explained urban space not as an invariable stone but a field of interactions among people that changes in accordance with collective and individual use, as well as experience.

Elena Ostanel (2013: 107) asserts that public space in places of difference could represent a "comfort zone" for some categories of city users while at the same time it could be perceived as stranger for others; she analyses this experience in her investigation of the square in front of the railway station in Padova (in Northern Italy), where the informal partition of uses made by dwellers or external city users is different from that of immigrants.

Through a qualitative analysis based on monitoring activity, Ostanel realises that residents experience the space as a "Non-place" (Augé 1992), which reflects its function as a place of transit, as opposed to the immigrants who use the square as a site for socializing and meeting, making it a "comfort area".

This example is suitable for understanding the relationship between people and space and the relevance of the appropriation dynamics, above all in cases where the social mix is very high. In general, people's approaches to public space create symbols, routines and uses that are comfortable; in cities where the level of ethnic concentration is high, there is a significant symbolic construction in order to feel at home. In places characterized by immigrants' presence, a "break of territoriality" (Yiftachel 1990: 340) can occur due to an intensive use of the space (Briata, 2014: 76), by business[5] providing foreigners with useful services.

Urban studies literature is full of investigations which recognize that proximity in public space is not enough to create social integration. Thus, it is important that urbanism poses strong questions in order to develop strategies that reinforce well-managed space. For example, who are the users of public spaces? In which places do people interact? Does interaction work, and why or why not? Which elements should be taken into account by urbanists in order to design spaces and institutions with an intercultural point of view?

6. Interculturality in urban planning

Many authors agree that contemporary cities should be more inclusive and adopt an intercultural approach in urban planning to overcome the diversity gap and attain multiculturality. The first model requires appropriate governance at each level and in different sectors, and it differs from multiculturalism in that it attempts to promote constructive interaction among people and groups of different backgrounds and cultures. Conversely, multiculturalism stops at the respect and mutual understanding of diverse cultures and considers identity to be a permanent concept. Interculturalism maintains that individuals and collective groups change constantly depending on the environment they live in.

Interculturality has been the challenge of the Intercultural Cities Programme[6] led by the Council of Europe, which supports public bodies in designing policies built on intercultural integration and considers diversity an asset for economic, social and cultural development.

---

5 Generally, immigrants tend to set stores up take away food business, transfer money services or phone centres.

6 "Council of Europe", 2018 (https://www.coe.int/en/web/interculturalcities/home)

In practice, all municipalities engaged in the project review all areas of policies included urban planning with the aim of ensuring equity, cohesion and non-discrimination.

As a result of increased migration flows, and in part inspired by the network of the intercultural programme, other cities in the world are becoming open to intercultural urbanism and try to integrate the diversity of communities into the planning and design of more attractive spaces for people of different cultural backgrounds. Another important component is the competence of urbanists in managing diversity, who should have knowledge of all forms of difference existing in the city and have a clear idea of who the users of that space are. Furthermore, they must account for the beliefs, behaviours and traditions of culturally diverse groups. In fact, intercultural competence is the ability to decode the mix of cultures and thinking in order to formulate constructions and urban spaces that are flexible and adaptable to diverse users. A strong intercultural place maker should know that listening and collaborating with minority groups is the most important aspect for success in planning. Co-production is fundamental to fostering citizens' shared ownership of spaces through participatory activities that allow people to exchange their opinions, express needs and interact with others.

Public spaces present a challenge for planners to create places that promote intercultural values through facilitation methods, such as forums and workshops between experts and citizens of different cultural identities. Within this framework, there are various examples of how cities plan new public spaces by breaking down issues of migration and diversity with the guidance of expert place makers, above all with regard to urban parks as spaces that can act as a field of dialogue and engagement. Inside the network of European intercultural cities, the interesting case study of the Ukrainian city of Melitopol's redesign of Gorki Park into an intercultural park is an example of the implementation of policies in which methodology is the most important element of the process: the development of ideas derived from groups of citizens working together with landscape architects and urban designers by attending workshop and meetings. After one year of workshops, the international team implemented ideas towards a renovated park for every kind of culture present in Melitopol through specific artistic sites, symbols, flora, traditional and intangible activities.

While substantial attention is focused on public space design, there is also a small portion of urbanists who are reflecting on mainstream housing planning, which is sometimes unsuitable for the needs of immigrant clients. Different cultures have different styles of living according to their behaviour and traditions. For example, Muslim people cannot have toilets facing the direction of Mecca, and many cultures prefer separate rooms for women and men or more bedrooms to accommodate large families, in addition to the various religious requirements that urbanists should bear in mind.

References

Augé, M. (1992). *Non-Lieux, introduction à une anthropologie de la surmo-dernité*. Paris: Le Seuil.

Balbo, M. (. (2015). *Migrazioni e piccoli comuni*. Milano: FrancoAngeli.

Bollier, D. (2014). *Think Like a Commoner: A Short Introduction to the Life of the Commons*. New Society Publishers .

Bottini, F. (2010). Questo libro: perché. In F. Bottini, *Spazio Pubblico – Declino, Difesa, Riconquista* (p. 13-17). Roma: Eddiesse.

Briata, P. (2014). *Spazio urbano e immigrazione in Italia Esperienze di pianificazione in una prospettiva europea*. Milano: FrancoAngeli.

Cancellieri, A. /. (2012). *Tracce Urbane Alla ricerca della città* . Milano : FrancoAngeli .

Carmona, M. (2010). Contemporary Public Space, Part Two: Classification. *Journal of Urban Design* (15), 157-173.

Carmona, M. (2010). Contemporary Public Space: Critique and Classification, Part One: Critique. *Journal of Urban Design* , 15, 123-148.

Carr, S. e. (1992). *Public Space.* New York, US: Cambridge University Press.

Council of Europe Ministers of Foreign Affairs. (June, 2008). *White Paper on Intercultural Dialogue "Living Together As Equals in Dignity".* F-67075 Strasbourg Cedex, Strasbourg.

Croso Mazzuco, S. (2017, July 28). Tratto da LabGov – Laboratory for the Governance of the City as a Commons: http://www.labgov.it/2017/07/28/public-space-collective-governance-and-the-urban-commons/

De Carlo, G. (2015). *L'architettura della partecipazione.* (S. Marini, A cura di) Macerata: Quodlibet.

De Carlo, G. (2013). *L'architettura della partecipazione.* (S. Marini, A cura di) Macerata: Quodlibet.

De Certeau, M. (1984). *The practice of Everyday Life.* Berkley, USA: University of California Press.

Education Youth Culture and Sport Council. (November 26, 2014). *Draft Conclusions of the Council and of the Representative of the Government of the Member States, meeting within the Council, on a Work Plan for Culture (2015-2018) - Adoption.* 15319/14 CULT 126 AUDIO 66 MI 869 RELEX 907 STATIS 121, Brussels.

Elena, O. (2013). Zone di comfort. Lo spazio pubblico nella città della differenza Milano. *Archivio di Studi Urbani e Regionali, Vol. 107/2013,* 9-29.

European Commission . (September, 9, 2005). *A Common agenda for Integration Framework for the Integration of Third-Country Nationals in the European Union .* Brussels.

European Commission. (2005). *Communication from the Commission to the Council, the European Parliament, the European Economic and Social committee and the Committee of the Regions - A Common Agenda for Integration - Framework for the Integration of Third-Country Nationals in the European Union.* COM (2005) 389 final, Brussels.

European Commission. (2008). *Communication from the Commission to the European Parliament, the Council, the European Economic and Social Committee and the Committee of the Regions of 17 June 2008 – A Common Immigration Policy for Europe: Principles, actions and tools.* COM (2008) 359 final , Brussels.

European Union, P. O. (2017). *How culture and the arts can promote inter-cultual dialogue in the context of the migratory and refugee crisis.* Luxembourg .

Foster, S. R., & Iaione, C. (2016). *The City as a Commons.* YALE LAW & POLICY REVIEW.

Gehl, J. (2010). *Cities for People.* Washington, USA: Island Press.

Hardin, G. (1968). the Tragedy of the Commons. *Science, New Series, 162* (3859), 1243-1248.

Harvey, D. (2012). *Rebel Cities: From the Right to the City to the Urban Revolution.* London: Verso.

Jacobs, J. (1992). *The Death and Life of Great American Cities* (Edizione Originale: 1961, New York: Random House Inc. ed.). New York, USA: Vintage Books Edition.

Lefebvre, H. (2014). *Il diritto alla città* (Edizione Originale: 1968, Paris: Ed. du Seuil ed.). (A. Casaglia, A cura di, & G. Morosato, Trad.) Perugia, IT: Ombre Corte.

Lefebvre, H. (1991). *The production of space.* Oxford, UK: Basil Blackwell Ltd.

Madanipour, A. (2003). *Public and private space of the city.* London, UK: Routledge.

Madanipour, A. (2005). Public Space of European Cities. *Nordic Journal of Architectural Research , 18* (1), 7-16.

Norberg-Schultz, C. (1980). *Genius Loci: toward a phenomenology of architecture.* London: Academy Ed.

Ostrom, E. (1990). *Governing the Commons: The Evolution of Institutions for Collective Action.* Cambridge University Press.

Penninx, R. (Dicembre 10, 2014). Il governo dell'immigrazione nei piccoli comuni. *Conferenza Internazionale realizzata nell'ambito del Programma di Ricerca di Interesse Nazionale (Prin) "Piccoli comuni e coesione sociale. Politiche e pratiche urbane per l'inclusione sociale e spaziale degli immigrati"*, (p. 14-33). Roma.

Powell, J. (2015, June 18). *What makes a commons? Cities and the concept of 'urban commons'.* Tratto da University of Glouchestershire: http://

www.ccri.ac.uk/what-makes-a-commons-cities-and-the-concept-of-urban-commons/

Ragab Nora, M. E. (February 15, 2016). *Role of Culture and the Arts in the Integration of Refugees and Migrants Report*. Brussels: European Expert Network on Culture and Audiovisual (EENCA), commissioned by the European Commission to inform the work of this group.

Sebastiani, C. (2010). Politica: governo collettivo dei beni comuni. In F. Bottini, *Spazio Pubblico – Declino, Difesa, Riconquista* (p. 235-243). Roma: Eddiesse.

TAM Associati (A cura di). (2016). *Taking Care: progettare per il bene comune – Catalogo Padiglione Italia de La Biennale di Venezia, XV Mostra internazionale di Architettura*. Padova, Italia: Becco Giallo.

Union, C. o. (November 19, 2004). *Press Release of 2618th Council Meeting Justice and Home Affairs* . 14615/04 (Presse 321), Brussels.

United Nations – Human Settlements Programme (UN-Habitat). (2009). *Planning Sustainable Cities: Policy Directions – Global Report on Human Settlments 2009*. Earthscan.

United Nations, D. o. (2017). *World Population Prospects: The 2017 Revision, Key Findings and Advance Tables.* . Working Paper No. ESA/P/WP/248, 2017, New York .

Yiftachel, O. (1991, January). State Policies, land control, and an ethnic minority: the Arabs in the Galilee region, Israel . *Environment and Planning D Society and Space 9(3)* , 329-362.

Allievi, Stefano (2018): Immigrazione cambiare tutto, Bari: Laterza.

Augé, Marc (1992): Non-Lieux, Introduction À Une Anthropologie de la Surmodernité, Paris: Le Seuil.

Balbo, Marcello (a cura di), (2015): Migrazioni e Piccoli Comuni, Milano: FrancoAngeli.

Briata, Paola (2014): Spazio Urbano e Immigrazione in Italia Esperienze di Pianificazione in Una Prospettiva Europea, Milano: FrancoAngeli.

Cancellieri, Adriano/Scandurra, Giuseppe (a cura di), (2012): Tracce Urbane Alla Ricerca della Città, Milano: FrancoAngeli.

Caponio, Tiziana (2006): Città italiane e immigrazione Discorso pubblico e politiche a Milano, Bologna e Napoli, Bologna: Il Mulino.

Centro studi e ricerche IDOS in partenariato con il Centro Studi Confronti (2017): Dossier statistico immigrazione, Roma: IDOS.

Council of the European Union (November 19, 2004), "Press Release of 2618th Council Meeting Justice and Home Affairs ." 14615/04 (Presse 321), Brussels.

Council of Europe Ministers of Foreign Affairs (June, 2008), "White Paper on Intercultural Dialogue "Living Together As Equals in Dignity." F-67075 Strasbourg Cedex, Strasbourg.

Education Youth Culture and Sport Council (November 26, 2014), "Draft Conclusions of the Council and of the Representative of the Government of the Member States, meeting within the Council, on a Work Plan for Culture (2015-2018) - Adoption." 15319/14 CULT 126 AUDIO 66 MI 869 RELEX 907 STATIS 121, Brussels.

European Commission (September, 9, 2005), "A Common Agenda for Integration Framework for the Integration of Third-Country Nationals in the European Union ." Brussels.

European Commission (2005), "Communication from the Commission to the Council, the European Parliament, the European Economic and Social Committee and the Committee of the Regions - A Common Agenda for Integration - Framework for the Integration of Third-Country Nationals in the European Union." COM (2005) 389 final, Brussels.

European Commission (2008), "Communication from the Commission to the European Parliament, the Council, the European Economic and Social Committee and the Committee of the Regions of 17 June 2008 – A Common Immigration Policy for Europe: Principles, Actions and Tools." COM (2008) 359 final, Brussels.

European Union, Publications Office (2017), "How culture and the arts can promote intercultual dialogue in the context of the migratory and refugee crisis." Luxembourg.

Grandi, Francesco (a cura di), (2008): Immigrazione e dimensione locale Strumenti per l'analisi dei processi inclusivi, Milano: Franco Angeli.

Lefebvre, Henri (2009): Il diritto alla città, Verona: Ombre corte.

Ostanel, Elena (2013): "Zone di Comfort. Lo Spazio Pubblico nella Città della Differenza Milano." In: Archivio di Studi Urbani e Regionali, Franco Angeli, 107/2013, pp. 9-29.

Penninx, Rinus (Dicembre 10, 2014), "Il Governo Dell'immigrazione nei Piccoli Comuni." Conferenza Internazionale realizzata nell'ambito del Programma di Ricerca di Interesse Nazionale (Prin) "Piccoli comuni e coesione sociale. Politiche e pratiche urbane per l'inclusione sociale e spaziale degli immigrati." Roma, pp. 14-33.

Ragab, Nora/McGregor, Elaine (February 15, 2016), "Role of Culture and the Arts in the Integration of Refugees and Migrants Report. Brussels: European Expert Network on Culture and Audiovisual (EENCA)," commissioned by the European Commission to inform the work of this group.

Tumminelli, Giuseppina (2010): Sovrapposti Processi di trasformazione degli spazi ad opera degli stranieri, Milano: FrancoAngeli.

United Nations, Department of Economic and Social Affairs, Population Division (2017), "World Population Prospects: The 2017 Revision, Key Findings and Advance Tables." Working Paper No. ESA/P/WP/248, 2017, New York.

Yiftachel, Oren (1991), "State Policies, Land Control, and an Ethnic Minority: The Arabs in the Galilee Region, Israel." Environment and Planning D Society and Space 9(3) 329-362.

NEW MAPS FOR THE DESIRES
OF AN EMERGING WORLD

Ottavio Amaro and Marina Tornatora

1. Foreword

> "The drama that Vermeer sets up on his stage [...]. It's about some-
> thing very different, it's about the desire to understand the world:
> not the one regarding the domestic interiors, or from Delft, but
> the endless expenses in which merchants and travelers will ven-
> ture, bringing home beautiful objects and amazing stories. Some
> of them are attracted from the view, to others the imagination has
> been kidnapped, and the most acute minds of the Vermeer gen-
> eration, reflecting on them, learned to see the world in a new way,
> redefining its dimensions by proposing new theories and new sci-
> entific models extended at a macroscopic level, to the whole ter-
> restrial globe and, to the microscopic one, depths that began to
> reveal themselves in a drop of water or in a speck of dust. The ge-
> ographer refers on this"[1].

> "In that Empire the Art of Cartography became such a perfection
> that the map of a single province occupied a whole city, and the
> Map of the Empire a whole Province. Over the time these bound-

---

[1] Brook (2015) p. 91.

less maps were no longer enough. The Cartographer Colleges
made a Map of the Empire that coincided perfectly with it"[2].

The epochal changes speeded up by the globalization of new things,
technologies and knowledge, pose new questions and new paradigms
about the sense of places and the desire for their collective and individual sharing. Millions of people move in time and space, approached
and constricted by the technological progress, with outstanding speed.
In this context, especially the cultural heritage, art and culture, in their
tangible and intangible forms, become the protagonists of new social
and economic dynamics, assigning to the experience of the journey a
method of identification through the discovery of the world.

This involves all of the social classes, different generations, various
professional profiles and specific geographical areas. It is well known
that on national and international level there is an exponential and un-
stoppable increase regarding the demand of tourism, placing cultural
heritage on a significant position.

Obviously, this does not guarantee the qualification of the demand
and therefore the offer of quality in search for knowledge in its multiple meanings. Indeed, very often, the division between financial and
economic powers and the cultural systems as a characteristic of the
contemporaneity is the origin for the idea of a merchandized and fragmented tourism. Very often this means a reduction of the *knowledge* to
a simple *information*, places of fleeting glances described as 'hit and go',
where the local identities vanish because of the process of globalization.

The same sophisticated technological advances that characterize
the era that we live in, bringing the knowledge into a strongly virtual
dimension, end up being misleading and causing evident misunderstandings. *Google Earth* creates the illusion of traveling in places and
landscapes, thinking of simultaneously sharing time and space. Basically, in reality it immerses in a non-space, immobile, silent, out of
depth and any particular character: "Modernity has transformed the

---

2 Borges (1958) p. 84.

world into one huge space, into a single enormous map that comes in crisis with the end of modernity"[3].

This wide and totalized vision, facilitated by the invention of the web, comes into crisis when it clashes with the need for a new relation between global and local, between an overall vision and the perception of places in their most identitary characters. The 'knowledge of the world' today passes from the ability to get out of a touristic system that is projected towards exclusive economic interests, creating stereotypes and advertising iconographies that substitute real places. This becomes a fertile context for experimenting with more interactive instruments that do not conceal information, but bring out visions and stories, visible or invisible. Places are the result of overlapping, thanks to information and knowledge, hiding semantic topographies, relationships between physical and metaphysical, readings of different literary, scientific and historical texts.

2. Map crafting

What kind of maps correspond to this? Which is the figurative language that is more appropriate to describe them? Are the conventional geographic tools sufficient to perceive them? Which are the relationships that the map should communicate, in a knowledge that is not limited only to the visible, but recounts what you can't see at first glance? Answering these questions can contribute to the design skills of the architect regarding the transformation of the places as well as to the traveler observation, intent on satisfying the desire for knowledge. Quoting Franco Farinelli, it is necessary to "search for a genealogy of visions into the projects. Innovation is necessary for finding a system of relations between the map (that is the expression of geography) and the mind"[4].

---

3 Farinelli (2015).
4 ibid.

It is clear that cultural heritage in its material and immaterial dimensions needs not only information but also the formation of the cognitive experience, where space and time, memory and evocative sense of vision, are fundamental elements for new possible maps. More often the idea of traveling is linked to the desire to see – it can be said in a Corbusian sense – that cannot be separated from knowledge, real or imaginary, as in the nature of places, bringing the idea of knowledge back to the observer. Taking this in consideration, conventional cartography risks to create real concealments, hiding the real "places of the mind", the presence of the human traces with the real and imaginary entity inherent in every place.

The structure of tourist guides, for example, often tends to impose things to see into the places and cities – buildings, artworks, environmental and landscape presences – forgetting about many others. There is a comeback of the original guides, like the *Peutinger* paper or the equipment supplied by the first pilgrims, where the main need was to indicate the long roads of the Roman Empire or to point out the places of worship, considering the rest unnecessary, therefore negligible or invisible.

> "Representing the territory is already seize. Now, this representation is not a cast, but a construction. The first role of the map is to understand, then to act. With the territory, it divides its nature to process, product, project: and since it is also form and sense, there is a risk to be taken as a subject. Established as a model, endowed with the charm of a microcosm, it tends to replace the real. The map is more pure than the territory, because it obeys to the principle. It lends itself to every design that led to anticipation and which it seems to prove the lawfulness. This sort of *trompe-l'oeil* does not display only the actual territory to which it refers, but it may also give a shape that it is not. It therefore manifests the nonexistent territory with the same seriousness as the other, and this is enough to prove how it is good to distrust ".[5]

---

5 Corboz (1998) pp 185-186.

The history of the representation of the world is based on this dichotomy. Art and science have characterized it in a dualistic development, on one hand assigning it the role of constructing the vision of the world, on the other hand seeing it as a geographical instrument to orientate and identify things and places. This in a constant need to explore, to understand, to recount and to show the world, to be able to look at it "with the eyes of the gods" or, better, with the "point of view of the gods".

The dream of Icarus was that one to be able to observe the reality from bird's eye view. From the literary description of the cartographers, of the fantastic geographers[6], as witness in history to the parallel and dialectic evolution of the practice and thought of the representation of the territory and, therefore, of *geographein*, or "writing the earth", together with the philosophical one – conceptual, through technical and technological evolution. It is necessary to overcome the human limit of the partial, fragmentary and therefore selective vision of the eye and thus of the body. From the *Peutinger's* map through the imaginary cartography up to contemporary scientific topography, there is the need of a totalizing and all-encompassing gaze, capable to unite the knowledge with the sense of the existence, in its form and its relationship with the cosmos. Having this as a background it can be said that the representations in history indifferently float between *real* and *dreamed* representation, above all when the map is given the task of investigating scenarios that are part of an organic collective imagination in the history of thought and of humanity, in their character of exploring physical and human territories.

"The territory of fantasy is no less real than the real one, and the fantastic map is no less true than the real one, and yet there is a difference, and perhaps lies in the opposition between the use function and the production of function"[7]. The Eighth Century Mundi maps, the Thirteenth Century Ebstorf map, the Renaissance maps that can be

---

6 See Calabrese O./Giovandoli R./Pezzini I. (1983).

7 Ibidem, p. 9.

placed between art and the science of survey, the utopian descriptions of Thomas More, the physical representations of the Earthly Paradise or the reconstruction of Atlantis of Athanasius Kircher, the Treasure Island of Stevenson or the Lilliput of Swift, the cosmological visions of Yambo in 1906, the description of the city and the territory of Perla in the short story *The other part* of Alfred Kubin, the geographies of Giorgio De Chirico, Carlo Carrà, Paul Klee, can be read horizontally as a history of the representation of the territory, as a history of thought underlying the research for *geographein*, as a representation of the world and the cosmos that surrounds us.

"Governed by chance and caprice, the geography of fantasy, woodworm of the international cartographic order, digs its orifices in the maps of each Country. Those who rush along the deviant and intriguing paths, runs unsuspected risks, enjoys unheard delights and luxuries.[8] The "Manual of Places of Fantasy" is presented as a practical guide of the described places, complete with recommendations and advice for the travelers, through maps and localized territories, ready for use "as for any real journey".

3. Science, knowledge, and representation

Although starting from different points of view and assumptions, each representation can be understood as a fundamental element in the construction of the more general mosaic, constituted by the need for discovering and knowledge. It is no coincidence that in the *Cartography* of the *Encyclopaedic Dictionary of Architecture and Urban Planning* the maps of "fantasy of places" are mentioned as an evolutionary reality of cartography itself. The current scientific achievements in the field of mapping do not move, but rather simplify and facilitate the representation of the unknown and unexplored territories, far from concrete and material reality, leaving the need to expand the world in

---

8 Ibidem, p. 32.

imagination and fantasy unchanged. On the other hand we are witnessing the evolution of cartographic representation as a science of survey and knowledge of the world accenting their value in practical use in the system of social, economic and political relations.

In the Renaissance there are remarkable achievements in the field of cartography: the Leon Battista Alberti treaties, the famous Letter of Raphael to Leo X, as well as the zenith survey of Leonardo da Vinci for the city of Imola, represent important moments in the history of cartography. It is since the Eighteenth century that radical changes take place, in the field of detection and the way of seeing and conceiving the territory. In fact, the particulate topographic representation appears, that is a new way of seeing the territory, the cities and their value. There is a strive towards a process of an abstraction, where the maps surpass particularistic needs, often linked to the identity of the territory, to submit everything to the homogenizing and indifferent logic of the maps. Everything becomes subordinated to the measure and evaluated in terms of super structural values: economic, legal, political.[9]

These changes are dialectically linked to the double change on the cartography: the passage to a reading through abstract interpretative models, and the changes of the "points of view", the actors-authors of the map. From the interpretation perspective, cartography starts to privilege the theoretical-abstract model where the territory is subtracted from ocular observation; the naturalistic vision of the places is overcome, focused on analogical models, of similarity and correspondence between the represented and the representation. The contents are transmitted with words, symbols and graphics, thus with a development of a universal symbolic-conventional language. The value of the map is linked to the political, legal, and administrative use of the contents, making direct point of view of the places that becomes completely superfluous. This is also related to the dissemination of changes in the disciplines such as descriptive geometry. The development of two-dimensional scientific-mathematical views, which in opposition

---

9 See D'Alfonso (1987).

to the monocular perspective view, tries to infinity and enhance the abstraction and conceptualization of representation.

The second aspect concerns the points of view and therefore the actors-authors: the cartography is no longer the prerogative of geographers, architects and technicians; new roles emerge that analyze society through maps such as sociologists, economists, jurists and politicians. The contents of the cartographies are beyond the direct, personal and/or artistic-cognitive: they acquire a "state value", therefore architects or thinkers are not the ones that produce maps, but the "scientists" statesmen who have the task of accurately rewriting the vision of the terrestrial space with roads, bridges, rivers, mountains, buildings, etc. In other words, a process has been started with the central point in abstraction and detachment from the "real"; a process that finds its exaltation in the contemporaneity with the digital papers that have become a set of numerical relationships.

The construction of new contemporary maps, above all finalized on the divulgative value of use on the touristic plan highlighting the cultural heritage, moves within this evolution of thought, as well as the idea of communication and representation. This has been posed as one of the problems of the research[10] on "Tourism as an art of places"[11] for the Calabria Region. The whole methodological and content apparatus tends to construct a paradigmatic experience approaching a place and projecting it primarily in a vision, in a way to feel it and think it, therefore in a seductive imaginary that needs to get out of stereotypes

---

10 See the research, Smart City *Progetto ACI. SmarT per la costruzione della piattaforma di servizi e strumenti - INMOTO — INformation and MObility for Tourism* - MIUR, P.O.N. Research and Competitiveness 2007-2013, Smart Cities and Communities and Social Innovation Asse II — Sostegno all'Innovazione Azioni Integrate per la Società dell'Informazione Azioni Integrate per lo Sviluppo Sostenibile — UNICAL, UNICZ, consultancy UNIRC

11 *Il turismo come arte dei luoghi* it is also the title of a research started in 2005 with a design workshop on the topic *Il progetto dell'esistente e il restauro del paesaggio* held in Pizzo (VV) within the department DASTEC from Mediterranea University of Reggio Calabria.

and generalizing images dictated more by the news than by their own historical/geographical identity.

In the last decades, Calabria has experienced a condition of overturning its image, related to descriptive factors of reports on economic and social degradation. A real disintegration of its identity and self-awareness therefore occurred, with the consequent loss of its narrative and figurative capacity, of the possibility of representing itself through an authentic iconographic culture. Deficit of representation as iconographic deficit is seen therefore as a limitation in the ability to affirm the project as an organic moment of valorization of all its territory in the more general context of the South and the Mediterranean.

A partial vision has been privileged, that has essentially omitted the internal areas, focusing on the edge of the coastline, without perspective depth, compared to its profound nature, still authentic in its historical and landscape conformation. The structural changes are added to this, since the 1960s, have distraught the connotations and the social, economic, cultural, as well as the territorial references.[12] These have made a real concealment of the identity of the places, overlapping history and nature in an indifferent way, constructing in the collective imagination the diffused and negative sense of an aesthetics of degradation.

4. Mapping Calabria

The project for new maps for Calabria[13] starts from the necessity to resume the sense of an interrupted story, able to bring out, almost like an archaeological unveiling, values and evocative visions of a region that regains its status as a historical-artistic *tòpos* to strengthen its

---

12 It refers to the failed industrialization that has created new ruins on the entire coast, the abandonment of agricultural culture, therefore of the internal areas, the emptying of urban centers through emigration, which has disintegrated the social and cultural fabric of the region.

13 The Thematic Maps are result of the research THE TOURISM AS ART OF PLACE, co-ordinated by Ottavio Amaro and Marina Tornatora within the research Laboratory

own identity in the more general context of the global 'journey'. In this framework the map, together with its use value, aims to create not only the figurative representation of the reality, but above all a "place of the mind"[14], the revival of an idea of territory that goes beyond the real/imaginary relationship, confronting the desire, the discovery, the evocative story, a property of the region. To it we can assign not only the descriptive value aimed at revealing itineraries, but mainly the ability to arouse and induce travel, to recreate the seduction of the traveler's own errand.

Starting from this, the construction of the new maps has favored a diagrammatic story, where the analogic representation disappears giving space to the abstraction that is more evident as a theoretical and mental conception of the territory than as a practical use-descriptive value. The map goes beyond the physical and illustrative narrative, opening up to the immaterial and the possibility of a multiple vision where the unpredictable, the seduction of discovery but also of losing oneself, become elements of attraction and multiform reading for the traveler. It is an approach that, starting from the contemporary technological development in the cartographic field, traces the ancient sense of the itinerary. As in the medieval maps of the first pilgrims, able to immerse in a journey characterized by the religious sense and the transcendent, and therefore from the evocative and above all purifying value, the meaning of the new maps is to recount a story made of episodes, steps, objects, descriptions, imaginary extensions of places.

Even in this case the first maps possessed an abstraction, privileging points and nodes beyond their connecting spaces. These maps are not intended to reproduce the world but to interpret it, giving more tools to those who use them; As J.-L. Rivière (1983) claims, "more abstract the image is, more the journey is concrete"[15]. The elaborations

---

LANSCAPE_inPROGRESS of the Mediterranea University of Reggio Calabria. The Research Team was formed by F. Arco, A. De Luca, G. Falzone, M. R. Caniglia, P. Mina
14 De Seta (2014).
15 Rivière (1983). p.20.

proposed in this text refer to thematic maps reviewed in their rigorous setting of partial and quantitative contents, to act as a hybrid condition of more information, 'visible' and 'invisible'. They escape from a codified apparatus of a conventional notational system, as the necessity for a reading on different scale, to search for its own language. The diagrammatic drawing represents the most effective form for contents that are not only iconic but also literary and conceptual. The eight thematic sections identify as many maps where the abstraction of the representation correspond narrations, possibility of deeper gaze on the treated places. We can discuss about maps of invention, of narrative devices, of attempts to search alternative maps:

1) The iconography and the journey

Richard Keppel Craven, Françoise Lenormant, Edvard Lear, Chatelet, Dominique Vivant-Denon, Henry Wisburne, Georg Gissing, Horace Rilliet as well as Norman Douglas, Escher, Guido Piovene, Pier Paolo Pasolini, starting from the Grand Tour, represent itineraries and points of view of the regional territory, still not 'contaminated' or 'polluted' by the publications of commercial tourism. They should be seen in double value: on the one hand as the narrative of a journey carried out in the morphological and landscape folds of a still wild and raw territory with a strong sense of individual discovery and with the anxiety of the unpredictable; on the other hand as the possibility to observe, through the iconographic and literary heritage left by travelers, a mirrored vision, where the symbology or the conventional and silent system of the map don't select the observation, but the eye and the gaze strongly connected to time, to the feeling and cultural relations of the observer.

Map 1. The iconography and the journey

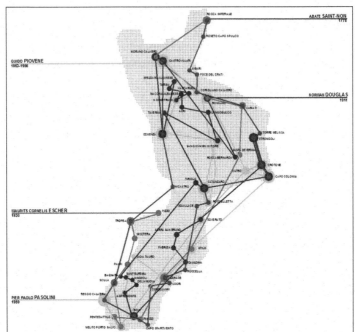

2) The literary narrative

It is a map that identifies the places lived by writers and poets, impregnated with their physical (dwelling, foundations, museums) and immaterial presence, steeped in a literary and poetic narrative, that is often the mirror, more authentic than reality, capable of penetrating in the *genius loci*, in the culture, in the anthropological depth of the places and people. Corrado Alvaro, Fortunato Seminara, Mario La Cava, Leonida Répaci, Saverio Strati, Adele Cambria, Enzo Siciliano, poets as Franco Costabile, Lorenzo Calogero, distinguished Calabrians, as well as Cesare Pavese, Giuseppe Berto, Norman Duoglas, Umberto Zanotti Bianco, Giuseppe Isnardi, have observed places, cities, landscapes, cultures and common people and then described them in a literary transposition, that outlines an ideal plot bringing out the research of seduction on the part of travelers. The strong bond created between the writer, the place and the story in many cases gives rise of real "literary parks", identifying the places lived by the writer or the poet and imbued with the charm of the stories.

Map 2. The literary narrative

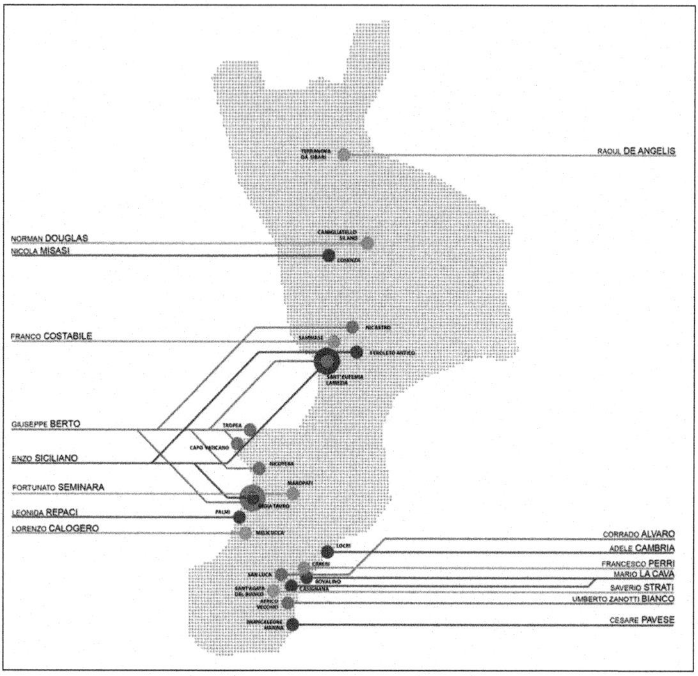

3) The places of mysticism

The map rediscovers the millennial internality of a land like Calabria, that in its roughness, very often inaccessible, still holds the charm of silence and mysticism. They are places of saints and hermits, of dozens of convents, hermitages and sanctuaries where since the Medieval and Byzantine age the history of religion and sacred texts have been rewritten. The Abbey of San Giovanni in Fiore, the *Codex Purpureus Rossanensis*, preserved in Rossarno, The Sanctuary of San Francesco da

Paola, the Certosa of Serra San Bruno, the Sanctuary of the Madonna di Polsi in San Luca, the places of Cassiodoro in Copanello, those of Tommaso Campanella in Stilo, of Barlaam in Seminara, identify the place of Calabria far from the noise of the coast and dedicated to mysticism and spiritual recollection of strong symbiosis with the landscape and the nature.

Map 3. The places of mysticism

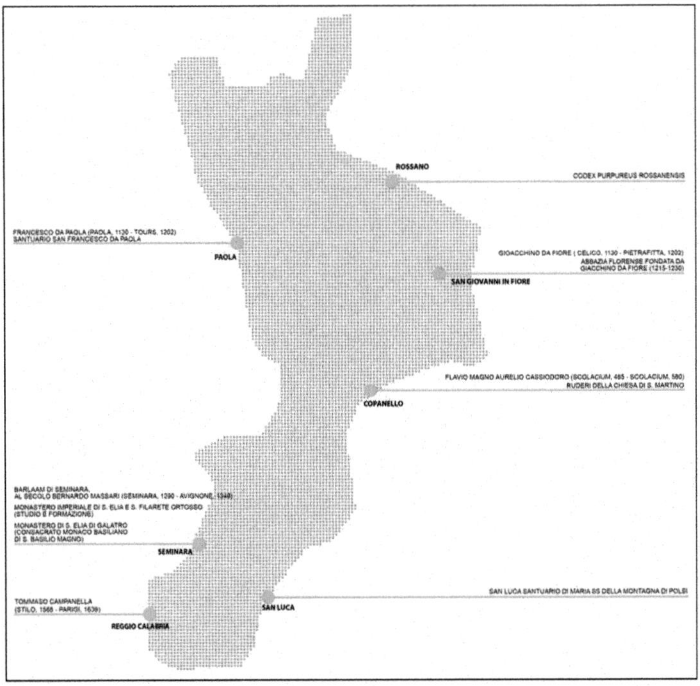

4) The places of art

This map unfolds along a twofold trail: the preserved art in museums, as well as the art disseminated in the landscapes: a new palimpsest in dialectic with the natural *icon* of the Region, a new interpretation of the original landscapes. Over fifty museums surveyed all over the Re-

gion, hosting ancient, medieval, modern and contemporary art, create
a cultural network of artistic heritage accessible to travelers. If on one
hand the art is an immense and universal form of knowledge, on the
other it is a discovery of the places in symbiosis with the landscape and
the ground on which it insists. The MuSaBa Foundation in Mammola,
the Bilotti open-air museum in Cosenza, the contemporary installations in the Archaeological Park of Scolacium, the contemporary signs
traced in the walkways of the abandoned city of Pentedattilo from VI-
ARTIS[16], these can provide travelers with new and rich interpretative
keys of Calabria.

16 Reference is made to the research work on VIArtis – *sulle rotte del Mediterraneo*,
conducted under the POR CALABRIA FESR 2007/2013, ASSE V – Natural Resources, Cultural and Sustainable Tourism. It intervenes in the field of contemporary
art through an interdisciplinary relationship between art, architecture and music with experiments and project interventions on some places in Calabria. The
results are reported in Amaro O. (ed., 2013), *ViArtis. Sulle Rotte Mediterranee*. Catalogue of Creative Sites, vol. I, Rubbettino, Soveria Mannelli.

Map 4. The places of art

MUSEO COMUNALE — PRAIA A MARE
                    FRASCINETO — PINACOTECA COMUNALE ANDREA ALTANO
                                        MUSEO DI ARTE SACRA
         CASTROVILLARI
MUSEO DI ARTE SACRA   MUSEO DELLE ICONE E DELLA TRADIZIONE BIZANTINA
MUSEO CIVICO SANTA MARIA DELLA CONSOLAZIONE — SARACENA   CASSANO — MUSEO DIOCESANO DI ARTE SACRA
MUSEO FRANCO AZZINARI   ALL'IONIO
                              ALTOMONTE
                                                                    CASTELLO DUCALE
                          CORIGLIANO   MUSEO DIOCESANO DI ARTE SACRA
                          CALABRO
                                    ROSSANO
MUSEO CIVICO "MARIO MORELLI" - CARLO LEVI   SAN MARCO
MUSEO BEATO ANGELO   ARGENTANO
MUSEO CIVICO DI ARTE CONTEMPORANEA SILVIO VIGLIATURO   ACRI
                                    BOCCHIGLIERO   MUSEO DI ARTE SACRA
MUSEO CIVICO
MUSEO DELL'ARTE DELL'OTTOCENTO E DEL NOVECENTO (MAON)   RENDE
MAB (MUSEO ALL'APERTO BILOTTI)
GALLERIA NAZIONALE A COSENZA
                                    COSENZA
MUSEO DI ARTE SACRA   ROGLIANO   SANTA SEVERINA   MUSEO DIOCESANO DI ARTE SACRA
                                                          MUSEO CIVICO CASTELLO ARAGONESE
                                                CROTONE   MACK - MUSEO PROVINCIALE
                                                          DI ARTE CONTEMPORANEA
                                                          PINACOTECA CIVICA
MUSEO CIVICO DI TAVERNA "MATTIA PRETI"   TAVERNA
                                                          MUSEO DI ARTE SACRA "SILVESTRO FRANGIPANE"
MUSEO DIOCESANO   ZAGARISE
                          LAMEZIA   CATANZARO   MARCA - MUSEO DELLE ARTI DI CATANZARO
                          TERME   MUSEO DIOCESANO D'ARTE SACRA
                                                CASA DELLA MEMORIA MIMMO ROTELLA
                                    GIRIFALCO   COMPLESSO MONUMENTALE SAN GIOVANNI
MUSEO DELLA TONNARA   TOLONE AZZARITI COLLEZIONE
                          PIZZO   ARCHIVIO DIOCESANO
MUSEO DI ARTE SACRA   SQUILLACE   MUSEO DIOCESANO
MUSEO CIVICO DIOCESANO RACCOLTA   TROPEA
PRIVATA TORALDO DI FRANCIA
                              VIBO VALENTIA
MUSEO STATALE DI MILETO   SERRA SAN
                          MILETO   BRUNO   MUSEO DELLA CERTOSA DI SERRA SAN BRUNO
MUSEO DIOCESANO PROVINCIALE DI ARTE SACRA   MONGIANA
PINACOTECA PROVINCIALE DIOCESANA   NICOTERA   MUSEO DELLE REAL FERRIERE BORBONICHE
                                    BIVONGI   PINACOTECA A.M. INTERNATIONAL DI BIVONGI PIU LABORATORIO
                          POLISTENA
MUSEO CIVICO   STILO   PINACOTECA FRANCESCO COZZA
CASA DELLA CULTURA LEONIDA REPACI   MAMMOLA   MUSABA PARCO MUSEO SANTA BARBARA
                          PALMI   OPPIDO
MUSEO DIOCESANO   MAMERTINA
                                    GERACE   MUSEO DIOCESANO DI GERACE
MUSEO ARCHEOLOGICO NAZIONALE
PICCOLO MUSEO S. PAOLO   REGGIO
PINACOTECA CIVICA   CALABRIA
                                ARGHILLA'
PARCO MUSEO ALL'APERTO
DI ECOLANDIA
MUSEO ALL'APERTO   PENTEDATTILO

5) The places of cinema

The map traces locations of many movies and documentaries from important Italian directors produced in the territory of Calabria from the 1930s until today. The cinema, as an acquired language of the modern and contemporary vision, has become a powerful tool for knowledge and representation of places. It often builds and invents the imagery of places. Its evocative power, poetic and descriptive, is certainly a very effective reading key also regarding the tourist attraction. Therefore, retracing the places of the cinema means pointing at possible unpublished itineraries, where lived memories are mixed (of actors, directors, etc.) with the scenes and the specialized captures of the camera.

Vittorio De Seta's documentary *In Calabria* of 1993, *The Gospel according to Matthew* of 1964 by Pier Paolo Pasolini, *The thief of children* of 1992 by Gianni Amelio, *Black Souls* of 2014 by Francesco Munzi express a vision of the landscape not as a background for the scene, but as a protagonist, in strong relation with the stories and the narrative and existential plots of the movies. To the literary story and the iconography of travelers, the project adds the dynamics of the cinema that insert the real element of people's life, often impossible to extract from the maps.

Map 5. The places of cinema

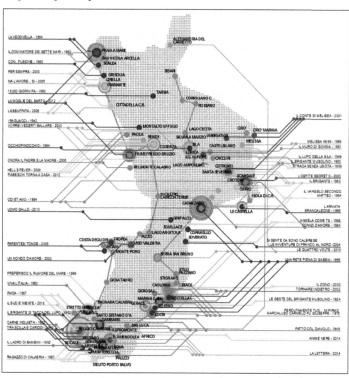

6) Desecrated lands

It is the map where events of crime, episodes of illegality and organized crime are intertwined with the history of many municipalities and geographical areas. Spaces of violence, itineraries extrapolated from texts such as the David's *Desecrated Lands*, or *The Hell* by Giorgio Bocca, trace the paths of knowledge and awareness of one part of the history of places. "In one of the most beautiful places of creation where the sky is clear and the sacred plant of the olive tree covers the soft earth with a silver roof, associations of thieves and murderers have sown death and destruction"[17]. If these are the places of tragedy, next to them are those of redemption and civil reaction, as the itineraries of the confiscated lands and labor camps of the Association *Libera*, destination for travelers who follow the maps of ethical and civil redemption with the activities of the community and voluntary service.

---

17 Bocca (1992) p.91.

Map 6. Desecrated lands

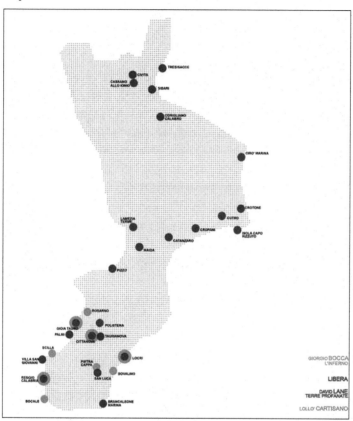

7) The places of classical archeology

It is the map that presents the cultural richness of a Region that has seen the interweaving and the contamination of different, distant and autochthonous identities. The condition of backwardness and isolation that has characterized Calabria for a long time, has paradoxically kept the whole cultural and archaeological heritage especially in the relationship with the ground and the landscape. The map identifies the archaeological parks, the network of museums, the historical landscapes, where it is still possible to discover the evocative meaning of the historical memory and the existence of different civilizations. While not preserving evident monumental vestiges, archeology constructs an important moment of writing on the ground as imprints of the city, especially from the Greek period, that are presented as real outdoor atlases of the ancient city. Locri Epizefiri, Kroton, Kaulon, Sibari, Shylletion, Medma, Vibo Valentia, Taureana, are some of the cities of classical archeology, where, since immemorial time, the relationship with the landscape still maintains the same seduction as on the Grand Tour travelers in search of the myth, the origins and the sources of Western civilization.

Map 7. The places of classical archaeology

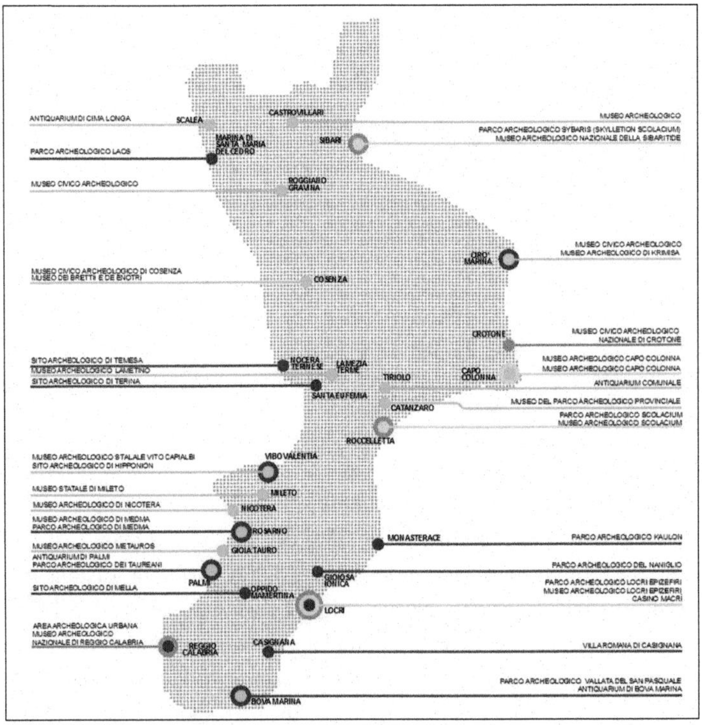

8) The great ruin

It is the map of a region rich in history and culture, related to continuous catastrophic events that have destroyed cities and monuments, cyclically bringing it back to the initial stage of its existence. Calabria, together with the topics of myth and history, becomes part of the European imagination through the image of the catastrophe. The urban imprints of the Greek cities, the temples of Marasà and Caulonia, the Cyclopean walls of Vibo Valentia, hundreds of single-aisle Byzantine churches, the Certosa of Serra San Bruno, the great dome of the convent of San Domenico in Soriano, The Ferriere and the Mongiana weapon factory, dozens of abandoned urban centers, the medieval castles and convents, construct the landscape elements of the "great ruin".

In the contemporary collective imagination, the ruin has a double meaning: an interpretative discovery of artefacts and monuments of the past, an evocative and poetic fragment in itself, capable of transferring and suspending history and memory on a more metaphysical and timeless meaning.

In such a respect the ruin acquires a specific value, establishing a relationship between the landscape and the context, as all the historical iconography has done starting from romantic time, where "the balance between nature and the spirit represented by the building in that sense gave place to nature"[18]. Moreover, the map contaminates the idea of the historical ruin with the existence of contemporary ruins, without any evocative memory: the unfinished coastal housing system, the abandoned factories, visions of unfinished infrastructure, construct a new imaginary where perhaps there is predominance of the fascination and the seduction of the irrational.

---

18 Simmel (1992) p.103-107.

Map 8. The great ruin

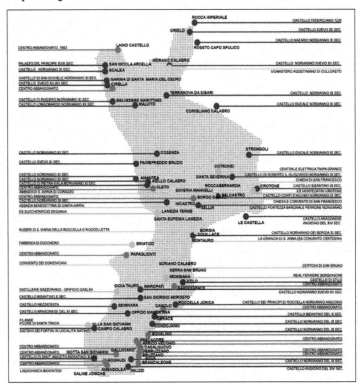

5. Concluding remarks

Next to the maps conceived as chapters of the same narration that moves in time and space on an eminently conceptual basis where forms and measures of the territory are lost, we crafted maps of the Region illustrating the parts that compose it more in detail: a mosaic/abacus that, as for any organism, describes the structural system that composes it. A long and narrow region like Calabria is characterized by a significant heterogeneity of the parts that compose it, which means a rich landscape, overcoming a simplified vision of the territorial uniqueness. Already in the past Calabria was distinguished in *Citerior* and *Ulterior*. In this context, the discussion is about landscapes in Calabria as dismembered parts belonging to a single body.

The new map is aimed to communicate this articulation, either on the nominal level or on the territorial level. It decomposes the landscapes of Calabria in relation to the morphological and territorial identities, identifying some *landscape rooms*[19]: areas in which cultural and environmental resources and assets are placed, in relation to their natural and historical context. Think about the tourist itineraries: their location within the *landscape rooms* connotes their historical specificity, the distances, the key for understanding a region that for years has lived in isolation from one *room* to another. Thus, a new identity map recounts the elements of the geography, but also the system of relations and interconnections that the region has experienced in its historical-cultural journey.

The map identifies fourteen rooms, tracked by many visions and points of view. As Guido Piovene noted in 1956: "Traveling in Calabria means to accomplish a significant number of roundtrips, as following the whimsical path of a labyrinth. Broken by those steep slopes, it is not only different from area to area, but it changes with abrupt passages, in the landscape, in the climate, in the ethnic diversity of the inhabitants. It is certainly the strangest among our regions"[20]. This applicative part of Calabria ended with the proposal of maps for rooms and then for itineraries regarding their interiors. The 'relativity' remains a problem of the map and of the risk that carries itself or in any case hides other truths and knowledge to the traveler.

It is the desire of making mistakes that characterizes those who travel, in the awareness of following often constructed 'labyrinths': "The most thoughtful and most significant cartographic 'text' remains the labyrinth: on one hand an 'author', a space, a limit, an itinerary, an end that can be death or liberation, on the other hand a 'sacrificed' who

19 See Purini (1991), and—with specific reationship to Calabria—Gambi (1978).
20 Piovene (1957) p.509.

must reinvent that space, that limit, that route, that end. Between the author and the sacrificed the challenge is supported by mutual solidarity, and mutual respect. Each of them does not know the other but perceives him; life is at stake, the itinerary is complete only if the sacrificed knows how to succeed from the labyrinth, as it has been prepared from the author"[21].

Map 9. The landscape rooms

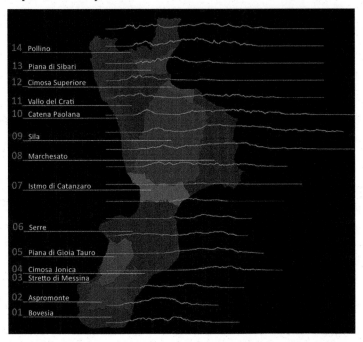

21 Macchi (1983) p.16

References

Amaro, O. (2013, ed.): ViArtis. Sulle Rotte Mediterranee. Catalogue of Creative Sites, vol. I. Soveria Mannelli: Rubbettino,

Bocca, G. (1992): L'Inferno, profondo sud. Male oscuro, Milano: Mondadori.

Borges, J.L. (1958): Viajes de Varones Prudents di Suàrez Mirando. Book IV, cap. XIV, quoted by Eco U. (1983): "Dell'impossibilità di costruire la carta dell'Impero 1 a l", in Calabrese O./Giovandoli R./ Pezzini I. (eds.): Hic sunt leones, Milano: Electa, p. 84.

Brook, T. (2015): Il cappello di Vermeer, il Seicento e la nascita del mondo globalizzato, Torino: Einaudi.

Calabrese, O./Giovandoli, R./Pezzini, I. (1983, eds.): Hic sunt leones, Geografia fantastica e viaggi straordinari, Milano: Electa.

Corboz, A. (1998): Il territorio come palinsesto, in Viganò, P. (ed.): Ordine Sparso: saggi sull'arte, il metodo, la città e il territorio: Milano: Angeli, pp. 185-186.

D'Alfonso, E. (1987): "Rappresentazione cartografica e veduta: l'opposizione tra ordinamento e immagine", in Quaderni del Dipartimento di Progettazione dell'Architettura del Politecnico di Milano, vol. 4.

De Seta, C. (2014): L'Italia nello specchio del Grand Tour, Milano: Rizzoli.

Farinelli, F. (2015): interview in www.igiornaledellarchitettura.com: October, 9th: International Summer School di progettazione architettonica e urbana OPEN CITY, Piacenza: Politecnico di Milano

Gambi, L.(1978): Le regioni d'Italia, Calabria, vol. 16, Torino: UTET.

Guadalupi, G. (1983): "Brevi cenni di geografia fantastica ad uso dei viaggiatori e delle persone colte", in Calabrese O./Giovandoli R./ Pezzini I. (eds.): Hic sunt leones, Milano: Electa, p. 32.

Macchi, G. (1983): "L'immagine impossibile", in Macchi, G. (ed.): Arte e scienza per il disegno del mondo, Milano: Electa, p. 16.

Piovene, G. (1957): Viaggio in Italia, Milano: Mondadori.

Purini, F. (1991): "Un paese senza paesaggio", Casabella, 575/576.

Simmel, G. (1992): Die Ruine, italian translation in Menozzi, L./Maniaci, A. (eds.): Le rovine dell'immagine del territorio calabrese, Roma: Gangemi, pp.103-107.

Rivière, J. (1983): "Itinerari", in Macchi, G. (ed.): Arte e scienza per il disegno del mondo, Milano: Electa, p. 20

ENTERING THE VOID
DIALOGUES ON ART AND URBANITY

Arthur Clay and Monika Rut

1. Introduction

Although many say that life is an adventure, our daily existence seems riddled with things that are unadventurous. These less adventurous moments range from waiting for an elevator, being stuck in a traffic jam, or simply being in a state of mind which is the result of wishes not yet fulfilled. To better describe these wearisome hum drum moments in life, the subject of waiting is looked at in this chapter by examining the places where these moments manifest and the state of mind that accompanies them. Novel solutions for cutting down periods of waiting or to distract a person from that fact that they are waiting are looked at with the goal of discovering how such "voids" are born and how they might be used to more positive ends. The chapter therefore poses the question as to what a void is and subsequently sets off an enquiry as to whether a void is something given and that we can find, or it is something that we mentally generate ourselves. Given that most of us find ourselves in voids, generated internally or externally, this chapter explores both and examines how these moments of apparent emptiness can be used to create experiences that somehow fill a void to the point that it simply ceases to exist.

Using a set of examples from historic tours, the motivations behind such tours, as well as the effects of traveling on the traveler are examined in order to reveal those moments in which there are potentials for voids to form. A comparison between the parameters of each of the tours – in terms of what is common and not common between them – is made to uncover the most important parameters of the voids encountered and how these parameters compare when cost and method of travel changes. Once a practical language to address the void has been established through examining the example set, recent practices of making use of voids by artists focusing on the creation of public artworks will be looked at in order to discover how known voids such as waiting for public transport to arrive, the distance between two places of interest, or simply a period of time during which one is forced into doing nothing can be exploited.

In order for us to come to a better understanding on how today's communication technology is enabling such artistic practices and how these can be linked to an emerging field of virtual tourism as part of the offerings in the repertoire of city marketing, the work of Virtuale Switzerland, a festival for invisible arts, is looked at in depth. This will show how curators of art events in public space are now able to make use of and even create such voids, which provide the ideal platform to experience the city on the one hand and the artwork on the other. In end effect, the combination of virtual arts and tourism for a collaborative bond with the mutual goal to increase the aesthetic wealth of the city at the same time reduce the number of uneventful moments with new and fulfilling adventurous ones.

Figure 1. Signs with QR codes and instructions offer easy access to art works at places of installation where potential viewers can expect a period of waiting. This type of access makes use of a given "void" where people naturally seek something to entertain themselves with while they wait for the ferry to arrive and bring them to another port on Lake Lugano.

2. The Voids of Existence

2.1   What is a Void?

To begin, it would be good to simply pose the question as to what a void actually is. For an answer, at least a temporary one, we might respond that a void is a space that we find ourselves in by circumstance that is best characterized as a state of being trapped in a situation that appears useless and which demands that one simply wait. However, it is important to note that there are many kinds of voids, but not all of them can be discussed within the scope of this chapter. Such voids as those created by the inducement of opiates, by daydreaming during a conversation and having missed out on a discussion, or the void that we enter when we sleep and completely disconnect from the world are not really the voids in which we feel a sense of emptiness and which produce a range of negative emotions. Belonging to the same group are also spaces that are physically void because they contain nothing, are not occupied, have been deserted, or are just spaces where idle avails.

The above-mentioned voids differ from the mental voids that we create and which we suffer from, through the negative emotions that the situation generates and which we allow to overtake us. However, there are of course ways – either through mental mastery, creative spatial design, or intelligent use of the arts – which could make the situation tolerable or help us gain control over it and manage it in such a way that we no longer experience the situation as a void. For example, a person in a stupor of waiting caused by an all too early arrival at a bus stop or train station in contrast to a person in the same void who happens to be able to focus on something that has a certain sense of wonderment such as glancing at a young women waiting for the bus for her date to arrive. The former is a void and possesses little magic, while the latter is one that seems to be filled with wonderment which the imagination gives birth to.

It is difficult to answer the question as to what a void is. However the first hint at what dissolves a void was brought with the example of the girl waiting for her date to arrive, because it points to a moment in which our imaginations become active and we take on the role of observer.

2.2   The Psychology of the Wait

One of the key elements that make void a void – meaning a period of time that is perceived as vacuous and in which nothing significant is going to happen – is the fact that voids seem to always involve a period of waiting. Of course, waiting is a common thing that most people do on a day-to-day basis, which can mean a wait from a few minutes at a bank machine, or one lasting a period of several hours at a voting booth. Rather than the mere fact that we are waiting, it is what we experience during that waiting that defines a void as an experience rather than a moment in which nothing is being experienced. The experience of being in a void can cover an array of emotions. It is the emotional experience that is in focus here, because it is a direct way to refer to the topic of the void as the "psychology of the wait", which is appropriate due to the fact that the number of emotions while waiting are many as they are varied.

Figure 2. The image depicts a "fake" Metro Station that was set up in Grand Central Station in New York for the purpose of offering the public virtual travel to Zurich. The station not only acts as a prop for making selfies, but serves as an entry point to a collection of AR works. People in the station are drawn to the Metro Station out of curiosity and this in turns dissolves the void they are in and offers them "a way out" of it through their curiosity.

Out of all of the negative emotions that a human is capable of experiencing, it can be said that none have been left out from a situation in which one is forced to wait. During any period of waiting, it is not only the fact that we experience emotions, but also that the emotions we are experiencing will come and go, alone or in combinations, and do so at intervals that seem to cover the gamut from long and static to short and chaotic intervals. For a better understanding of this, imagine the following situations which are heavily characterized with strong emotions: a person having anxieties about his or her relationship while their partner is away, or any situation that appears to be unfair such as when someone cuts into the waiting line. These experiences are not necessarily bad *per se*, but they are judged as being negative, because they possess unknown factors, which are always a key source of impatience and are therefore negative.

2.3 Coloring and Shaping the Void

In computing languages there is a 'wait' command that is used to put a process on hold until the execution of another process operating in the background has ended. Applied to the situation of waiting for a human, the longer a person has to wait before moving forward with their plans, the opportunity to make use of the wait with another activity grows. Of course, this is provided that what a person is doing in "the background" while waiting is something of value – which, when we measure the frustration associated with waiting, this is often not the case. So if we continue to keep the wait command in mind and apply it on the level of human activity, we discover that most of us are constantly trying to fill the meaningless void of existence with something meaningful. However, our inability to transcend the void keeps us on hold from doing something which we might wish to do and which we find meaningful.

Figure 3. A screenshot of the AR Artwork "We AR Butterflies" produced by Virtuale Switzerland with the artist Arthur Clay for the Science Museum Seoul, South Korea. The work is an example of how Selfies can be used in a way in which visitors can interact and join in the creation of a work

2.4   Forging a Connection

It was inferred above that an intelligent use of the arts could be adopted as a method for eradicating voids. It is also true that artists are
masters at describing and depicting the voids as humans experience
them. For example, the film "Enter the Void" (2009) written and directed by Gaspar Noéi defines what a sense of emptiness is by depicting
human existence as a meaningless void that is filled with more mean-
inglessness through the choices people make on how to spend their
time. The film, staged under the neon glow of Tokyo nightclub signs,
uses a wide range of cinematography effects and well-chosen music
tracks to transform the banality in the lives of the characters into a
poetic expression that turns emptiness into wonderment. The director describes the film's subject as "the sentimentality of mammals and
the shimmering vacuity of the human experience". Noéi's ironic use of
words, such as describing vacuity as shimmering, tells us of the transforming powers of the creative imagination in coloring and shaping
the voids of human existence.

In the same vein as "Enter the Void", is Timothy Leary's "The Psychedelic Experience" published in the 1960s. Taking the same approach
as in the film "Enter the Void", the book mimics the contents of the "Ti-
betan Book of the Dead" with good intent, hoping to provide a simulation of death and rebirth with the idea to 'liberate' human beings
from the problems in life caused by the chain of mistakes made, and
complicated by the futile attempts to solve them. The potentials of the
void are not only revealed at the levels of arts and literature, but also
at mundane levels of the everyday. Both the film and the book – if not
most artworks in general – suggest that a deeper sense of being must
be discovered. As proposed by the content of the above examples, it
seems that such a result can only be achieved through reality-bending
substances that lead to greater sense of harmony, suggesting a parallel
between the arts and drug state can be drawn because both nurture
the bending of reality through a change of perspective, offering us the
way out of a void through the use of the imagination.

2.5   Occupied Time and Non-Occupied Time

To begin to understand how the arts can add meaning to the voids and
eliminate them, two examples, drawn from the history of architectural design, will suffice. In contrast to the psychotropic cinematography
of an art film mimicking drug-induced states or of a book describing
outer body experience, a simple example of how a void caused by waiting can be eradicated is the well-known and widespread use of a mir-
rors placed adjacent to an elevator will do. A well-placed mirror allows
us to wander with our eyes, to look at ourselves, to look at others, tidy
ourselves up, and even spy on those behind us. Another example of this
is the well-known wait at a bus stop, which has been 'shortened' by simply providing information monitors that offer a time schedule. Even if
these systems are not technically perfect and don't offer precise arrival
times, they do serve their purpose as mechanism that psychological-
ly shorten the waiting time. Having a general idea of when a bus will
arrive – whether accurate or not – is comforting to those waiting. In
end effect, people are also more positively inclined to make use of the
service in the future.

Everyone knows that time passes faster when you are doing something while waiting. So we can conclude that it is not the waiting that
needs management, but the situation in which it takes place. Simply
put: every waiting queue is a problem, but every waiting queue is also
an opportunity. So, the answer to our question as to what void is and
how it can be eliminated lies in the opportunity offered by the void,
which entails not insisting on a shorter period of waiting, but in providing more engagement while one is waiting.

Keeping the situations described above in mind and how the voids
were eliminated, one realizes that the opportunities presented by voids
can be seized to eliminate the negative experience associated with
waiting and taken to express something that is creative and meaningful and actually reverse the situation into a positive experience. Being
made aware of solutions such as the placement of a mirror, encourages
us to use our imaginations and to search for and find ways to dissolve

voids, which are capable to provide meaning while we are engulfed in vacuity. Certainly, if we are successful in finding solutions to voids and we are able to provide meaningful alternative to waiting, we can take advantage of the opportunities that are provided by voids when we travel, when we meet others, and during those moments when we find ourselves waiting for something else to happen.

Figure 4. The three of the most celebrated travel routes in European history: The Grand Tour (left), the Kangaroo Route Tour (middle), and the "Hippie Tour" (right)

3. Tourism: Roots and Reasons

3.1 Pleasure and Business

From one perspective, tourism is basically traveling for pleasure and from another it represents the business of Cities and Countries, which will always involve strategies for attracting and succinctly accommodating and entertaining tourists. Although tourists can be defined in general as people who are traveling to reside in places outside their usual environments for short periods of time, however the purposes for them doing so varies. Pleasure is of course a central motivation, but traveling can also be motivated by reasons of health, leisure, and even business. Interesting enough, tourism has a long history, which includes travels at the domestic or at the international level and therefore a major source of income for both Cities and Countries alike. Tourism not only determines the branding image of a place, but it ultimately determines to a large extent the living standard of a City. In turn,

tourism contributes to creating the image of City or Country, it also
determines the character and atmosphere, of a place, which in turn
attracts tourists as well as future residents and, more importantly, it
contributes to the sales of domestic products.

*Table 1. The table shows similarities and differences between the three
most famous tours from pre mass-tourism. All of the tours covered
distances of great lengths and all of them where undertaken with the goal
of experiencing people and places that lay outside of the normal habitat
of the traveler. Interesting to note is that in terms of itineraries, only the
Hippie Tour was left open to chance and not dominated by either a clear
itinerary nor limited to closed group of select people,. The Grand Tour and
the Kangaroo Route were organized professionally with hired staff, but the
Hippie Tour was organized solely by those traveling and in contrast to the
immense amount of planning common to the other two tours, spontaneity
was the key factor that determined the scope of the tour.*

TOUR	TOURIST ROLE	TUTOR ROLE	AGENT ROLE
Grand Tour	Tourist	External (Private Person)	External (Private Person)
Hippie Tour	Tourist	External (Chance Encounters)	Internal (Within the Group)
Kangaroo Tour	Tourist	Internal (Personal)	External (Private Company)

Although the Grand Tour was a trip undertaken by mainly young up-
per-class European men whose main destinations were those centers
where the cultural legacy of classical antiquity could be found and
studied, it is interesting to note – and this will become an important
subject in this chapter – that modern tourism can actually be traced
back to the Grand Tour. Of course the Grand Tour included a diverse
range of activities which, along with traveling to distant points, also
included viewing works of art, learning new languages, experiencing
diverse cultures, tasting different cuisines, and mingling with others.
All of the above were integral aspects of the Grand Tour and each aspect
branched out over time into what we refer to as niche tourism today.

Although mass tourism of today appears contradictory to the undertakings of the Grand Tour, it does stem from it. Mass-tourism came about with the advances in technology, making it possible to transport large numbers of people in a relative short time span to distant parts of the planet. This development was a key factor in enabling those with limited means to enjoy the benefits of leisure time outside of their normal domesticity. However, with the diversification of clients and offerings, mass tourism continued to grow but began to split and separate into smaller and more intimate categories of travel, having particular goals in mind. As mentioned above, such forms of tourism are termed niche tourism today and refer to any form of travel whose focus is narrowed to a specific activity.

3.2   Filling gaps with voids

Turning back to aspects of the Grand Tour, it is important to note that the primary focus of it was the pursuit of cultural experience. If a comparison can be drawn with the Grand Tour at the level of mass tourism, the categories of tourism that have retained some aspect of the cultural endeavors of the Grand Tour would be Heritage Tourism and Cultural Tourism, both of which are forms of niche tourism that specifically focus on culture.

Heritage tourism is a branch of tourism oriented towards exposing cultural heritage at the location where tourism occurs and this includes experiencing the places, artifacts, and activities that authentically represent the history of the location and the culture of its inhabitants; cultural tourism, with its roots in the Grand Tour, is arguably the original form of tourism. It is concerned mainly with regional culture, specific to the lifestyle of people in those geographical areas one is visiting and can include tourism in historic city centers and areas and cultural facilities such as museums and theatres.

It is important to note that cultural consumption habits of Europeans include visiting museums and concert halls abroad almost as frequently as they do at home, and because of this both heritage and cultural tourism are the forms of tourism that many policy makers are interested in as a form of tourism for the future. This is also due to the fact that both forms of tourism allow the city to portray itself and do so with branding that reflects the city with integrity. The movement towards these forms of tourism underlines the growing importance of cultural tourism as a source of cultural consumption and also gives reason to why institutions mandated for tourism are now consistently viewing such as an important potential source of tourism growth.

It is clear that cultural tourism is 'good' tourism. It attracts high spending visitors and does little damage to the environment or local culture while contributing a great deal to the economy. In contrast, there is also concern that cultural tourism might do more harm than good, because it allows too many tourist to penetrate sensitive cultural environments, adding to the complexity of their upkeep and perhaps even influencing their life span. The situation however opens up space for change and innovation. For example, the use of virtual technologies has brought in an array of possibilities, which allow visitors to experience sensitive cultural environments through AR and VR setups. The approach not only cuts down on time spent at sites of cultural heritage, but it also allows for more visitors to experience those sites as well as providing promoters with better ways to inform and educate tourists about what they are viewing.

The end results of these endeavors is to be akin to the goals of the Grand Tour, where the traveler seeks enrichment through the exposure to culture. Interestingly enough, the technology involved here is so breathtaking in its use of imagery and media that it brings us back to the phantasmagoric approaches in Enter the Void and The Psychedelic Experience. Equipped with the electronic enhancements used in tourism today, tourists find themselves immersed in virtual worlds, traveling less through physical space and more through the use of our imaginations.

Table 2. Route comparisons between real three real tours and a virtual tour. The chart introduces and compares methods of travel, numbers who traveled per year, the duration of the travel, and the distance covered. Comparing the historical tours, it can be discovered that over time longer distances were traveled with shorter periods of time and that the between time taken and distances traveled is ironically restored to the ratio of the Grand Tour with the Virtuale Tour. This suggest that with the advent of new technologies a new era of tourism in which more can be seen than meets the eye and which the "traveler" despite the short distance travels to discover and experience things outside of his or her normal everyday habitat.

NAME	GROUP	CLASS	BEGIN	END	GOAL	METHOD	YEARLY	TIME	DISTANCE
GRAND TOUR	Alone	Upper	London	Rome	Educational	Horse Carriage	Hundreds	Years	1435 km
HIPPIE TOUR	Small Group	Middle	London	Bangkok	Spiritual	VW Bus	Thousands	Weeks	9525 km
KANGA-ROO TOUR	Diverse	Middle	London	Sydney	Leisure	Jet Plane	Millions	Days	17000 km
VIRTUALE	Diverse	Diverse	Basel	Basel	Diverse	Diverse	Thousands	Hours	10 km

3.3   Digital tourism: more than reality in your hands

Augmented reality, or AR as it is commonly abbreviated, is a technology that allows us to augment a real-world environment with computer-generated media, fitting in well with the more general concept of "mediated reality", in which any aspect of reality is modified by the intervening powers of a computer. In contrast to virtual reality, AR does not attempt to replace the real world with a simulated one, but functions by enhancing one's current perception of reality. Augmentation is conventionally applied in real-time and in a semantic context together with what it proposes to augment. Uses are extensive and range from enhancing sport shows with vital information and expressive graphics to artworks that immerse the viewer into phantasmagoric worlds that are brought to life through the creative expression of an artist. Advances in AR technology are increasing and the ability to add the use of computer vision and object recognition to place augments is leading to highly interactive and digitally manipulable environments.

With tourism having to focus more and more on cultural themes and sustainable models, the advances in AR technologies brings about new forms of niche tourism that embrace mediated realities. It is hardly a surprise, that as new technologies develop and are linked to today's network communication systems, that both sides of tourism are offered an immense array of new possibilities. Clearly, a new era of experiencing reality through the lenses of technology is born, allowing tourism to not just be part of the real world but to successfully link to the virtual worlds, which explore heritage in new and innovative ways that are able to cope with demands of mass tourism.

This is accomplished using mostly mobile phones and tablets and although the displays of these seem small because they are designed to fit easily into a user's hand, the effects of immersion common to AR transform the small screen into a looking glass of grand proportions. So, in many ways, our handheld phones and tablets have become our travel ticket to much grander worlds. With the creation of public artworks that make use of the places where they can be seen, visitors are allowed to go beyond what can be seen with the naked eye and fill the voids of existence through expressing the products of the imagination which mankind has celebrated over centuries with the use of creativity. The constraint of having to hold a device out in front of you at all times may be the price we pay for traveling, but then again that is not much to ask if a completely new world is opened up to us.

Figure 5. A comparison of the route of the Grand Tour and the route of the Virtuale Route through the city of Lugano. The Grand Tour route (right side of image) often began in London and ended in Naples after traversing through Belgium, The Netherlands, Germany, Austria, and Switzerland. The comparison between the Grand Tour with the Virtuale Lugano Route shows thatn both routes are designed as routes with multiple stops of interest which when combined offer a particularly diverse and cultured experience.

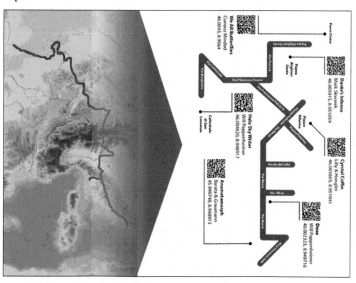

3.4   The Grand Tour and other legacies

With the information provided above it is now easy to see that the effects of the concept of the Grand Tour have spread over time and are now taken up by tourism industry. So contrary to what one might think, the legacy of the Grand Tour actually lives on into modern times. It is of course no longer reserved for those of privilege, but still plays its role as a form of rite of passage and remains a source of inspiration for all artists and art lovers alike. Whether by plane, train, boat, car, bike, or on foot, the richness of travel becomes self-evident – if not through personal experience during trips then in those works of art and literature that depict it. For example, think of what we can experience in works like "On the Road" by Jack Kerouac (1957) or "Into the Wild" by Jon Krakauer (1996). In these and other works of the same genre, the contact between the elements of our world and ourselves come together in meaningful experiences ranging from the adventurous – the free-spirited blissfulness of traveling in an open ended truck through America against a backdrop of jazz, poetry, and drug use, to the tragic – Thoreau-like journey to the Alaskan wilderness of super tramper, Christopher McCandless that ended in his demise in an abandoned bus at a point on the Stampede Trail.

Figure 6. A tour map showing the five routes in Basel named after famous individuals from Swiss history. The map shows that many stops along the routes include important monuments and buildings that characterize the city. The circular images indicate where along the routes the works could be found.

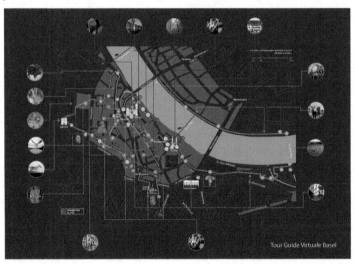

3.5 The Hippie Tour

Obviously, the idea of travelling for the sake of curiosity and learning is an idea that was developed in the Seventeenth Century, and the endeavours inherent in the Grand Tour reappear to us in the novels of Kerouac and Krakauer, where the goal of the traveler is to open oneself up to experiencing a sense of life through the act of traveling. As time moved forward and the idea or concept of the Grand Tour made its way through the lenses of time, permutations of it evolved and were adapted by those interested in traveling as a form of cultural enrichment and as a sort of rite of passage. Although it cannot be said that the offshoots that follow mimic the Grand Tour, but starting in the 1950s many Westerners began to travel a route between Europe and South Asia, which in time became to be known as the 'Hippie Trail'. It was named after the counterculture of the times whose embracement of alternative lifestyles, cultural diversity, and social experiments that are now assimilated factors in the mainstream society of today.

The Hippie Trail typically started from cities in western Europe, often London, Copenhagen, West Berlin, Paris, Amsterdam, or Milan and then ran down mainly through Iran, Afghanistan, Pakistan, India (including Jammu and Kashmir) and Nepal. In contrast to the costs associated with the Grand Tour, the Hippie Trail was a form of alternative tourism, and a key element of it was travelling as cheaply as possible in order to extend the length of time away. In terms of the tour acting as a rite of passage, those taking it focused on finding opportunities for interacting with the local population and not on "wasting time" on visiting tourist attractions. This new trend combined well with the methods of traveling which included hitch-hiking, cheap public and private forms of transport that traveled the route. This resulted in the sharing of ideas and experiences which nurtured counterculture and was in part responsible the social revolutions of the 1960s, inspiring the creation of such works as "Enter the Void" and the "The Psychedelic Experience".

3.6   The Kangaroo Tour comparison

The Kangaroo Route is yet another established travel route that gained a similar status as the Hippie Trail. Traditionally, it refers to air routes flown by Qantas Airlines between the United Kingdom and Australia via the Eastern Hemisphere. Like the Grand Tour, it was an undertaking for the wealthy due to the cost of flying small charters to rare places. With very few exceptions, the route involved travelling by small aircraft seating fewer than twenty passengers, used many intermediate flights of local airlines and making use of strange and out-of-the-way airfields. Unlike the large vessels of today's mass tourism, the experiences offered by traveling with small aircraft was one of flying low and slow, which was received enthusiastically by those undertaking the trip, simply because it offered the opportunity for sightseeing from above and frequent rests at unusual stops. Although it was consuming and expensive undertaking, for the traveler it was filled with far-away and hardly known places and therefore attractive to those seeking personal fulfillment through travel.

4.   The birth of the virtual

4.1   The Communion of Communication Technology

The success of any city marketing (or institution representing that city and which therefore is part of that city's offerings) will depend solely on their abilities to communicate their real as well as their virtual offerings properly to the public. Today's tourists are now to a large percent digital natives, born and bred in virtual worlds, who come with expectations and are no longer that acceptable or as easily excited with being presented with solely real things. Important cultural attractions, for example museums, are now using digital tools to market content to visitors, and city marketing offices in the area of tourism are following suit with new ways to make sightseeing experiential by adapting paradigms already known and practiced in electronic urban arts. For those who have already familiarized themselves with the potentials in recent changes in technologies, it is no longer the real object itself that holds the public's interest, but what it is virtually linked to.

This tendency can be seen in how the blending of the virtual and real is able to create a unique and contemporary experience for visitors. This not only includes changing commonly accepted logic with which cities are marketed, but also entails adding new layers of interest to that what is already present through the use of virtual arts, digital heritage, and even urban gaming.

The genres mentioned above are all hybrids between real and virtual, which let visitors actively experience what a city can be today, what it was yesterday, and perhaps what it is becoming in a not all too distant future. The adoption of the approach of mixing the real with the virtual using today's communication technology allows a city to go beyond what is apparent and brings marketing strategies to not only entertain and educate their guests, but also to show how tourism can be made to adapt to the demands of the time. Soon, tourism will be able more than actually is physically present and will be able to adapt more quickly to needs by using real time data which are generated through participation. This means that it will be possible to nurture a tourism that contains the cultural breadth of a Grand Tour by adapting new public arts, the intimacy of a Hippie tour through a personal and experiential approach, and the potpourri of a Kangaroo route through the diversity offered by the flickering between real and virtual worlds. Such "hybridating" could clearly lead toward a tourism that is less prone to consumerism and more supportive of sustainable city marketing.

4.2   The Virtual in Action

Clearly, the arts spawned by the electronic revolution in communications technologies at the end of the Twenty-first Century with the advent of the smartphones have allowed artists to harness the virtual to create artworks that overstep the boundaries of exhibition space (galleries, museums, etc.) and which have expanded into the domains of unbound urbanity, where they flourish in the heart of the city and fulfill the interests of a tech-smart Twenty-first Century audience, who yearn for the new and unique that is found in the virtual arts and who are at the same time interested in sensitizing themselves to the cultural heritage of the city.

Unlike the arts of previous centuries, the virtual arts of today are able to be forthright present and all pervading, because of the use of mediated technologies that allow for a dialogue between what is present in reality and what is overlaid virtually. For example, artists using Augmented Reality techniques have been able to present a variety of contemporary themes directly to the public through immersive experiences, which join knowledge sharing with aesthetic experience in uniquely effective ways by simply designing the works to be experiential and site specific.

Table 3. Table of AR Artworks plotted to categories of Niche Tourism, connecting then to aspects of the tradition to the Grant Tour.

WORK	ART	MUSIC	FOOD	HERITAGE	GARDEN	WATER	FILM	LIT	ARCHI	POLITIC	ME
Money Can Buy You love				X		X					
My Mirror City				X					X		X
Things We Have Lost						X					X
WiMet Spinners	X										
Dante's Inferno	X			X							
AR Butterflies											X
Mushrooms on Tour	X					X					
The 4th Dimension	X							X			
Sense of Place Breslau				X							
Butterfly Lovers	X			X	X						
TotenTanz		X		X					X		
Diamonds Are Forever	X		X						X		
Biomers Skelters					X					X	X
Radio Heads				X				X		X	

Virtual arts in public space appear at a time in which many cities are joining campaigns on sustainability. In order to join in on reducing the carbon print and regulate and reduce waste while dealing with an ever-growing populace of inhabitants cities have to be marketed as culturally enriching both historically and as contemporary points of culture. Technologies today have helped for the better and are moving the agenda on sustainability forward and toward a more positive outcome while they communicate and market their offerings.

Figure 7. The artwork "Money Can Buy You Love was created by the arts group the Curiously Minded to celebrate the traditions of money trading and minting in the city of Basel. The coin was digitally minted to mark the 500th anniversary of Basel and new forms of currency such as the Bit coin. Touching any one of the coins opens up stop motion film created in a workshop for youth where goal was to use the coin to create social warmth with it.

The fusion of art and science is well known and has been practiced as a curatorial approach for over a decade with great success in museums. With the same level of intensity and appeal, virtual arts have been able to fuse with tourism to create new and unique ways of presenting arts and portraying cities. This has led to unique collaborations between city managements and artists which have resulted in the flourishing of a form of urban arts that embrace past histories at the spaces that they are presented in. This has brought changes to the general schema of event management and its logistics. For the Virtuale Switzerland – a festival dedicated to the virtual arts which presents projects in Digital Heritage, Urban Gaming, and especially artwork using Augmented Reality – this move forward has meant gaining the ability to install works anywhere and without the need for transport, insurance, or physical install at a location, reducing the carbon print as well as the circumvents restrictive laws when working in historical districts.

To prove the practicality and the potentials of the use of electronic arts as part of the tourism package, several cases studies will be presented taken from festivals held in Basel, Lugano, and Lausanne, which were produced, curated and executed by Virtuale Switzerland. These examples depict a diverse range of approaches in terms of how the Virtuale set up art tours that highlight the offerings of a city, which are conceived and implemented to flow through a city, in order to provide the proper setting for the artworks and make the act of visiting a city multifaceted and truly unique.

Individual artworks will also be brought as examples to show how AR artworks can link to heritage and culture while retaining their integrity as artworks. Such works range from static sculptures and monuments to immersive and interactive experiences, allowing the public to become part of creative act through personal involvement in shaping the artwork itself. If both the static and the interactive forms of such works are planned properly, the routes along which they can be seen enhance the offerings of a city and provide an interesting way for visitors to experience the city as timeless, meaning they can experience its history, its present state, and what might be planning for the future. This is made possible through the types of information that the artwork is able to present and how the visitors can then interact with it on a tactile level by navigating the provided channels.

It will also be shown how such an embrace of arts and tourism is akin to many forms of niche tourism, by fitting into new forms of tourism and evolving with them. Clearly, the traversing the routes formed by the placement of artworks reveal that connecting this form of arts and tourism truly fit into new and evolving standards of tourism, and offer new potentials in supporting a mass tourism that is sustainable. Further, the intensity of how visitors interact with an artwork can prove valuable to marketing institutions and help them come to a better understanding of how people are navigating the city, what offerings are appreciated, and how they can be better marketed (and therefore experienced) through digital possibilities inherent in the use of AR, VR, and MR systems.

Figure 8. A screenshot of the artwork "Biomer Skelters" by Will Pappenheimer and Tamiko Thiel taken in front of the Basel Rathaus which was installed along the Paracelsus" route in Basel during the Virtuale Switzerland Festival in Basel.

5. Arts and the City: Dialogues of Urbanity

5.1   Virtual Basel: routes and works

The Basel edition of the Virtuale Switzerland digitally enhanced the "Five Scenic Routes" which connect the two parts of the city known as "Grossbasel and Kleinbasel". The mapping of the five routes and how the artworks were placed along them, opened up visitors to those parts of the city which they might not have found on their own, or may have never thought of even going to them. One of the major factors in planning the placements was that each of the routes is named after an important person from Basel's history. The choice of whom a route was named after was well chosen by those who planned the routes at city marketing.

The "Erasmus", the "Hans Holbein", and the "Paracelsus" routes for example lead tourists through those older parts of Basel, where Erasmus von Rotterdam, Hans Holbein, and Paracelsus lived and worked. Following in the footsteps where they had walked themselves in the Fifteenth and Sixteenth centuries, visitors to the city are lead to both parts of Basel. The Hans Holbein route and the Jakob Burkhardt cross from Grossbasel over to Kleinbasel. In contrast to the Hans Holbein route, the Burkhardt route brings visitors to places that were built at later points in time and lay outside of the old city walls. These particular routes offered the festival the opportunity to make use of the ferries that cross the Rhine river and to place artworks on the water so that when viewers crossed over they found themselves immersed in the middle of artworks.

Each of the routes offered the public a different collection of artworks and all of the routes focused thematically on the person the route was named after. For example, Paracelsus. He believed that everything in the universe was interrelated, and therefore dedicated much of his life to finding beneficial medical substances that could be found in herbs, minerals, and various chemical combinations thereof. For a route dedicated to Paracelsus, it seemed appropriate to choose an artwork that actually put the viewer into a "mood" of healing, which was visually akin to the thoughts that Paracelsus was most likely having on the healing of human illnesses while he walked that very same route.

The work, titled "Biomer Skelters", was created by Will Pappenheimer and Tamiko Thiel as a participatory public artwork, which in the words of the artists "connected body rhythms to potential ecosystems". As festival participants walked the Paracelsus Route, a simple wearable bio-sensing system employed their heart rate to plant and populate their path with fantastic AR vegetation. The process described by the artists is one where "the interior energy of the body is the generator of a wake of wild growth that is left behind them as they make their way through the city". Although the work is in the form of an ecological "game", which was designed to focus on contested notions related to conservation versus possible climate transition, it is appropriate to the route. When we read how contested the views of Paracelsus were at the time, we feel while participating in the viewing of that work that we are being brought closer to emotional life of a great thinker and are giving our attention to ecosystem we live in.

Figure 9. The image depicts phases of Will Pappenheimer's work WiMet Spinners seen while traveling through it on the Metro between Flon and EPFL stations tops. Based on the interference patterns, the work is perpetually changing and those interested can explore the work time and again regardless of the direction the Metro is traveling. The public could QR into the work from a hanging advertisement poster. Although the void was not designed but a given, how the void interacts with the artwork over time is carefully calculated.

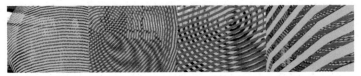

Another work that explored cultural heritage as a subject matter and which offered the visitors proactive involvement was the artwork "Money Could Buy You Love". It was created by Virtuale Switzerland as a contribution to the 500 years anniversary of the Rathaus. The work was placed in the Basler Rathaus, which is part of the Erasmus Route. To explore the meaning of the Erasmus Route and the person whom it was named after, efforts were placed on finding a concept for an artwork that embraced the ideas of Humanism and the production and exchange of currency. The theme of Humanism is relevant, because Erasmus was known under the sobriquet of "Prince of the Humanists". He asserted that humanity must take responsibility for its own destiny and believed that doctrines of theology should be derived from human needs and interests rather than from theological or ideological abstractions.

The production and exchange of currency was chosen as a second theme, because it celebrates the traditions of money minting and trading in the city of Basel. In order to match this theme with that of Humanism, a new coin was digitally minted to mark the 500th anniversary of Basel and to celebrate the birth of new forms of currency such as the Bitcoin. The digital coins, which were the central part of the work, were animated to appear as if they were falling from the sky. In this work, the engagement with the viewers takes place by prompting them to touch the coins as a gesture of "exchange". By doing so, nothing was purchased per se, but the person touching the coin in an act of exchange is greeted with one of a collection of stop motion films that was created in a workshop for the youth, whose goal was to use the coin to "mint" social warmth. Viewers watching the films were inspired by their inventiveness and were convinced that exchanges of 'value' could be motivated by other things than the need to purchase.

Figure 10. The image is a screenshot of one of many the AR works that was accessible through the QR code on the signage on the sides of the Metro Station. Once viewers scanned the QR code with their mobile devices, they had access to the MetroNext+ app, which allowed them to choose which artwork to view. The app included works by Arthur Clay, John Craig Freeman, Will Pappenheimer, and Lalie Pascal (Depicted).

5.2   Lugano & Lausanne

The other routes in Basel that have not yet been mentioned adopted a similar approach. However, festivals held in Lugano and Lausanne did differ: the tendency towards creating new ways to transverse the city by matching artworks with points of interest and by offering the public a new way to interact with their surroundings that were proactive greatly increased. The difference between the Basel, Lugano, and Lausanne festivals is important to mention so that the reader can better understand that the possibilities of linking artwork to city spaces can be done with much fantasy and can be done in a relevant way to the city's characteristics.

Unlike Basel, Lugano is a lake-side city. This characteristic of the city was taken up by offering tours for both the city as well as for the lake. For the tour that went through the city, the itinerary included important sights at diverse locations through out the city. Starting from the new Cultural Centre LAC, the tour continued down the long narrow of Via Nassa where most designer shops can be found, through the center of Lugano where visitors were able to discover the traditional and cultural aspects of the city. All along the way, visitors enjoyed viewing a fantastic array of new virtual artworks that matched the sights, or filled the voids between them as they walked from one to the next sight. Navigating upwards through narrow streets to the Cattedrale di San Lorenzo, visitors were confronted with something completely new: they could write wishes and wants in the sky using Will Pappenheimer's "Halo Skywriter" and have others see it by sharing it through their mobile devices or via social media. The route ended with an optional visit to the city's greenest area, Parco Civico, where visitors could make selfies and turn into butterflies in the work "We AR Butterflies" by Arthur Clay. The butterflies could then be seen by all with a mobile device as they flocked and fluttered through the park's gardens.

The tour for the lake was termed "Waters and Ports" and consisted of a route that brought visitors to all of the popular and charming ports along the lake including Museo Helvetia, Grotto Elvetia, Gandria, Museo Doganale, Caprino, and Saint Rocco. This was accomplished by working closely with the boat excursion routes from Società Navigazione del Lago di Lugano and the Unseen Art Festival of Australia. With these partnerships, the Virtuale was able to make use of the Lake area and exploit it in new ways with a collection of selected new artworks. Each of the works for the lake tour was placed at a port along the lake; as the boats neared the ports, visitors were able to see the artworks floating above the port while the boat was docking. While the boat passed through the middle of the lake, visitors found themselves immersed in a virtual field of colorful water lilies and under a star flickering sky in works by Tamiko Thiel and Warren Armstrong respectively. Although visitors had enough to take in as they crossed the lake and even while they were docking at the ports, the void resulting from having to wait for a boat to arrive, gave ample time for visitors to discover the artworks at the port while they were waiting.

Figure 11. "The Coming of a New Dimension" by Arthur Clay installed at Lugano Art Center during the Virtuale Switzerland Festival for Lugano, Switzerland

The Virtuale in Basel explored routes through the city and made use of the many bridges that connect Gross and Klein Basel; the Virtuale in Lugano contrasted the city and the lake with two different tours with contrasting sets of artworks. For Lausanne, a concept was developed to include the diverse parts of the city as was done in Basel and Lugano, but the opportunity was also taken to make use of Lausanne's new metro line. This approach worked well for city marketing, because Lausanne is now coined as the "the smallest city in the world with a metro".

Similar to the approach taken for the lake tour in Lugano, the Virtuale Switzerland developed a dedicated work for the both lines of the Lausanne Metro with the artists Will Pappenheimer. The artwork was titled "WiMet Spinners" and consisted of a suite of smaller works that

could be in eleven Lausanne Metro stations. Together, they connected
the center of the city to all possible places of interest in Lausanne including the Rolex Center at EPFL, where a separate group exhibition
was installed.

The artist described "WiMet Spinners" as a collection of leaking
network apparitions that can be characterized by groups of rotating
colorful objects and patterns that formed clouds of ephemera. Particular to this work and something which was first explored in Lausanne,
was to position one of the works in the suite in such a way that the
viewers could travel right through it as if they were the lens of a projec-
tor and the artwork was the film that was running over it. Although the
objects in the work were stationary, they appeared to be in perpetual
movement and because the work was based on interference patterns
it changed in imaginative ways from the beginning to the end as the
metro moved closer to and then finally through the work.

From the above depictions of the tours, the Virtuale Switzerland
was able to conceive and design routes that lead visitors through extended tours and bring them to celebrated points throughout a city
without being confronted with voids of ennui caused by waiting or
from walking unentertained. During all of the tours, visitors were not
only able to take in what was there in reality but were also able to experience a dialogue between the artworks viewed and the place where
they were being viewed. Proving that a city can be experienced on
both the real and the virtual plane and the combination between them,
brings a new dimension city marketing and to tourism in general.

5.3   AR Travel Gateways

The design of a route and the choice of the proper artworks to present
along it are two of the three important elements of creating a virtual
art path through the city. The third important element and the most
important and challenging is conceiving how visitors will be able to
access the artworks using their devices. Once a visitor has arrived at a
point of interest, there must be a clear and easy way for them to access

an artwork. Although this can entail simply giving them a URL link, a keyword to Google, or a QR code to scan in, the Virtuale has always gone to great lengths to make the process of "keying" into a work an interesting if not a fantastic event in itself.

At the beginning of this chapter it was shown how a QR code that is integrated into a visually appealing graphic and which is placed at a void can prove very effective in providing a gateway to an artwork. There are however other approaches to creating a gateway that actually contribute to the area where the artwork can be seen and which increases the impact of the artwork at the same time.

The eloquent example of a gateway that provides an interesting way to key into a work, was the "MetroNext+" project that was part of the "2016 Zurich Meets New York Festival". The MetroNext+ project was a joint collaboration between Virtuale Switzerland and ETH Zurich and was inspired by the Metro-Net projects of the German artist, Martin Kippenberger, the "MetroNext+" project undertaken by the Architect Christopher Clay and based on research done at the New York Public Library. The Augmented Reality experience that was created to accompany the "Metro-NeXt+" station consisted of two contrasting projects. The former was a set of floating Platonic and Archimedean Solids that were textured on the outside with subjects common to Swiss culture and opened up upon clicking into floating art galleries with works by renowned artists such as the Curiously Minded, HR Geiger and Lorenz Meier. The latter was created by using photogrammetry software from the ETH Zurich. Using the software it was possible to generate 3D model of the Swiss street scene from a very large number of photographs taken in historic part of the city along the "Augustinergasse".

To raise curiosity amongst members of the public, the curators at the Virtuale took up their interest in exploring the culture around the making of selfies. People passing through Grand Central Terminal were drawn to the MetroNext+ Station out of curiosity and then felt compelled to come closer and make a Selfie with themselves in front of it. Looking at the Selfies taken, the image gave the impression that the person in the photo were off to Zurich. Since, the QR code and the instructions on how to enter the exhibit were integrated onto the sides of the station, it was very easy to get visitors to the the MetroNext+ station to scan the QR code in and get them to view the works.

The MetroNext+ Station not only served as an entry point to a collection of AR works that could be seen in and around Grand Central, it was also a way for visitors to virtually visit Zurich where they could experience a selection of architecture, arts, science, as well as the lifestyle of Switzerland's largest city. The quote presented to the public clearly underlines the intentions of the project: "Hurry, get on board, it's comin'! Listen to those rails a-thrumming. Get on the NeXt train and find yourself where Zurich Meets New York!"

6. Conclusions, and beyond Conclusions

In order to bring this chapter to an end, it is necessary to return back to the concept of the void and the motivation to use it as a mechanism for fulfillment. This will aid the reader to make connections between the diversity of what was discussed and let them draw their own conclusions about the possibilities brought about by combining new electronic arts with the needs of tourism today. Cleary, we all experience voids and most notably when choices are limited by standards hindrances such as schedules and costs, but also from the outside world due to regulations or just circumstance. Perhaps, meaningfulness is found in our lives only when we actually undertake and realize the things that we imagine experiencing. However, we can in some way reach or obtain the things we desire through fantasy being powered by active imagination.

The artwork "The Coming of a New Dimension" depicts the descent of the Tralfamadorians, Vonnegut's fictional alien race from his book "Slaughter House Five" who had the ability to free themselves from the restraints of time and visit all moments in the past, present, and future as they desired, in order to rectify something that has happened by explaining it from a perspective that it simply does not matter. The work was created by Virtuale Switzerland with the authors of this article sums up not only the experience of the void as a psycho-dramatic moment that transcends reality by producing an intense feeling of immersion when viewing the work, but also inspires as Science Fiction does, to consider looking for solutions that are not imaginable or even possible today.

Even if nothing matters – as the Tralfamadorian Philosophy dictates – then perhaps even those moments of apparent emptiness that make our lives seem meaningless are then insignificant, because perhaps it is true that the determinism that is present in our lives through the stature we are born into can be circumvented by the use of the imagination. This is something that the artists in our society excel at, who exercise free will and use it to create experiences that somehow fill the voids to the point that they cease to exist, even if just for a moment that was imagined, dreamed, or part of another place that is virtual.

Certainly, whether our trips take place completely through our imagination, or through one of the many established travel routes of our times, we as travelers need to distinguish figure and foundation and seek out those places, real or virtual. Gilbert Simondon points the way to understanding this in his "The Essence Of Technicity", in which he states that the magical universe can be experienced, where the segregation of man and nature dissolves and through the reticulation of space and time we become privileged to a primitive mode and sense of unity. To paraphrase Simondon and make use of his concepts of unity to bring things to a close, we can state that the moments in which we experience the magical universe in ourselves, is when it becomes possible for us to discover where all of man's power of acting can be found and all of the capacity to influence the world is concentrated. Therefore, tourism as discussed within the framework above, inspires us while traveling not only to look outward at the wonders that society has brought, but also inward using our imaginations to enter the void as a form of rite of passage only possible with a synergy between real and virtual.

3. THE URBAN FABRIC BETWEEN INTUITIONS AND CONFLICT

ART AS A SOCIAL PERFORMANCE IN TRANS-MEDIA CITIES

Letteria G. Fassari

1. Foreword

The designing of contemporary cultural spaces needs to take into consideration the incessant expansive movement that affects reality due to the multiform and pervasive universe of the web, and the digitalization of social space. The implications of this transformation are numerous and not fully explored because change is underway. We know, however, that the representation of the world, which we experience through the media world, is a whole experience in itself (Lash 1999). This telluric movement also brings with it a more powerful implication highlighted by Žižek (1997)[1]: enriching the perception of the world with electronically grafted digital information, "augmented" reality reveals the phantasm, which serves its own construction. In this chapter we explore how social actors inhabit the excesses and the speed this change brings with it, and the actor's responses in ways of experiencing the trans-media world.

Looking at how social media effects have been interpreted, the aesthetic form of the *simulacrum* (Debord 1967; Baudrillard 1981) predominates. It refers to how actors implode in the simulation of the world, losing themselves as subjects. Here, the logic of the end and the disso-

---

1 http://www.filosofia.rai.it/articoli/žižek-il-rapporto-tra-lo-schermo-e-la-realtà/37954/default.aspx

lution of reality prevail. Instead we hypothesize that the way actors inhabit the worlds expanded by media is not *simulacrum* but *performance*. This means that the continuous acting out that we see flowing in trans-media storytelling can no longer be read as a loss of the self but rather as a non-cognitive position, yet affective, relational and sensorial, that ferries to a reflexivity that is mostly aesthetic (Beck, Giddens and Lash 1994). Through performance, meanings are formulated in a social and aesthetic rather than cognitive space, and the participants seem to be engaged through the imaginary in the interactional creation of reality (Korom 2013). We can find dissolution but also critique and resistance. We do not know if coping with the complexity of the world through performance is a desirable process but surely it must be taken into serious consideration in the cultural planning of new social spaces.

2. Life, form and revealed ghosts

Observing the social world in its making and unmaking means facing the Simmellian dynamics between life and form. We produce forms that are goods, technologies, ideologies, artefacts, buildings, paintings, sculptures, performances etc.; in their development these forms become objectified and return to the life that produced them as domination. Simmel speaks of *"verdichtung"* (crystallization) of forms that turn against life (Simmel, 1997: 5). Life, however, does not resign itself and systematically frees itself by returning to its vital flow. In this movement modernity is evolved and devolved.

The place where this movement is accelerated is, according to Simmel, the metropolis: display windows, artificial lighting, universal exhibitions, trams and cars, foreigners, the poor, criminals, objects and people with whom the metropolitan individual enters constantly into contact. The resulting shock causes a real anthropological change toward intellectualization at the expense of sentimentality: the coldness of society, which contrasts with the warmth of community.

Through intellectualization, the metropolitan individual abstracts from the personal dimension and re-establishes subjectivity in terms of calculation, reason and interest (D'Andrea and Federici, 2004). Walter Benjamin acknowledges the profound change of the early twentieth-century technological environment and gives medial substance to the Simmel form. According to Benjamin the experience of modernity is centred on shock, the motor responses of switching, snapping, the jolt of a machine in motion producing new subjectivities (Buck-Morss, 1992).

In radicalized modernity, aesthetically within the post-modern (Lash, 1999), the question of the convergence between media evolution and the processes of individualization intrinsic to modernity remains unchanged and is actualized in understanding how subjects and media are comprehended or given one to the other. If we look at contemporary social experience, it appears condensed in the gesture of stroking and the rapid passage of the fingers on the cold surface of smartphone screens; it appears to us as a hybrid of socio-technical entities and new imaginaries (Latour, 2005).

The assemblage of human and non-human actors engrossed with screens implies a reflection on their interaction and between these screens and the same living organisms. As McLuhan points out: "every invention or technology is an extension or a self-amputation of our body, which imposes new relationships and new balances between the other organs and the other extensions of the body" (McLuhan, 1962: 61). The concept of body extension in the medial environment indicates a real "process of morphing, resulting from the transfer of the flesh, the body of the individual into a larger mediascape" that inevitably dissolves the perimeter of the subject (Canevacci, 2007:17).

The bodyscape then seems to dissolve in the media environment and communication. I do not want to go further into this snapshot of everyday life that would take me directly into the areas of the post-human and its multifaceted implications. Instead, I choose to observe the aesthetic form assumed by the representation of social experience on

the threshold of the changes taking place, in short, the relationship between screens and reality.

Screening the world is embedded in a fundamentally ideal path
that challenges the representation of experience. Whereas modern-
ism had differentiated the roles of meaning, signifier and referent,
post-modernization triggers a process of de-differentiation among
these elements, making them interchangeable. An increasing proportion of signification is in fact relegated to images; these, as Scott
Lash (1999) writes, are more similar to referents than words. Likewise,
a growing proportion of referents is made up of signifiers. It follows
that everyday life is pervaded by a reality that increasingly includes
representations and in which a reciprocal invasion of signifiers and
referents is established. What we witness is an irreversible crumbling
of the regime of representation.

There is also a further implication on which I would like to reflect:
we think of ideologies as pre-digital devices mediating the relationship with reality, but as Žižek (2017)[2] underlines, especially in the most
recent technologies the screen filter has a different quality. What does
this mean? Žižek remarks that grafting data on reality and making
it immediately available – as google glasses do – reveals the cultural
construction of reality. In other words, it reveals how the construction
underlies reality. It is not only a process of delegation to the machine
but also a revelation of the phantasm through which reality can be interpreted (Žižek 1997).

The problem is then not technological change but the augmented
reality or the enrichment of human sensory perception through information manipulated and conveyed electronically; what we see through
the glasses is not just reality but reality with the addition of the phantasm which allows it to function (ibid.). Žižek exemplifies: "I see a
beautiful woman but I also process her erotic fantasies" (see footnote
1). The evolution of digitalization makes the construction behind the
perceived reality explicit.

2 See footnote 1.

Following the contribution of the authors considered, we are faced with a profoundly changed experience of reality with respect to the past. Is it possible to interpret this experience using the binarisms which define modernity: real/virtual, reality/representation, public/ private, cultural/ social, real/imaginary, etc.?

We certainly cannot answer these questions here but in exploring the possibility that these dichotomies are no longer pertinent to understand contemporary experience, we then ask ourselves how the social actors' response to change is being formulated. The hypothetical answer, for the moment more descriptive than interpretative, is that the responses of actors are a continuous performance (Gemini, 2003; St. John, 2008; Boccia Artieri, 2012) where Giddens' cognitive reflexivity (in Beck, Giddens and Lash, 1994) takes on another form transfigured into reflexive acting-out.

It may seem paradoxical but if we recall the status of performance in contemporary art we can understand that it is a "practice of movement" of subjects expressing languages and consuming at the same time. Performance is a strategy of positioning in the uninterrupted flow of communication in which objects, representations and symbols interchange. However this is not a closing in on themselves, because as we will see performance is always connected. As Duchamp would have said, it is the spectators who complete the work when they experience it.

3. Mimesis as aesthetic reflexivity

Modernity defines itself as reflexive when it begins to reflect on itself; reflexive modernization is a realization of one's own excesses and of the vicious spiral of destructive risks. While for Giddens (1994) this kind of reflexivity finds form and substance in the continuous implementation of processes of monitoring and processing of an essentially cognitive type, Lash (*ibid.*) expounds a critique of this one-sidedness and recalls the aesthetic dimension to support this reflexivity. In it a significant role is played by the particular and the contingent with respect to universals, to which cognitive reflexivity applies. Lash, among others, refers to the contributions of Adorno and Benjamin, or the tension to understand life in its symbolic, imaginative and irrational dimensions.

The way in which one enters the medial environment recalls the mimetic form of the relationship with the associated world and often above the cognitive one; following Tavani's take on Adorno, the aesthetic dimension produces relationships, builds connections and establishes instable grammars, without planning or predictability (Tavani, 2013: 47). The peculiar role played by mimesis refers to a new ecology of thought. Mimesis abstracts form, concept, from exclusive attention to unity and synthesis; it "deflects the technique in the direction of the removed, the widespread and the unstable" (ibid.: 139); mimesis introduces an element of otherness, openness, able to counteract the tendency of form to be closed.

Tavani shows us a less "apocalyptic" Adorno, equipped with a particular technological sensitivity (ibid.: 152). This sort of identification of the technique with the spirituality of the work, in fact, leads the philosopher to glimpse a margin of transformation even for art in the era of reproducibility. He admits the possibility that art works can move with "technological talent, in technology itself" (ibid.: 174). Mimesis, however, cannot be restricted to art, poetry, aesthetics but, according to Wulf (1995), mimetic sense plays a key role in acting, representing, speaking and thinking of human beings as significant conditions of social life.

The daily flow of the trans-media experience seems to be closer to this mimetic kind of "critique". Reflexivity is daily, experimental and above all it is the reflexivity of an aesthetic, emotional kind, transported by images, by their editing, by grafts of words and fiction, by a weaving that does not refer to cognition but to mimesis as a form of knowledge of the world. We are always within a process of appropriation of the image of the world (Abruzzese, 2001) and a retreat from the trust that others can represent the unique and singularized experience. The trans-media flow seems to testify to the continuous appeal for individualized stories. The hero's journey is not that of building a famous life of success but of a struggle to assert one's own singularity. This is not an epic but a performative struggle. The autobiographical, medial performance gives rise to monologues, the documentation of an individual life as research, a personal life that recounts its own conflicts and victories, and that the flow returns as a collective narrative but not collectively oriented. It is affirmed as testimonial logic and as a very personal position.

Performance as more mimetic than cognitive reflexivity is aligned as a response to the transformation of the world into image, first of all because it refers to the limits of theorization. Adorno considers mimesis a movement with which man gets lost in the "environment" (Adorno, 1975: 83; Wulf, 1995). According to Adorno the privileged environment in which mimesis rushes is art, but what we witness is the slipping of art into the social. In order to escape from ordinariness, anonymity, normality, individuals attempt to take artistic forms, using them to navigate the sea of communication (*ibid.*). Whether these are symbolic or simulacrum is not the subject of this essay. In any case it is a *connected* performance (Boccia Artieri, 2012), which is never solitary. In such a respect we welcome Wellemer's critique of Adorno, which considers aesthetic experience only in "ecstatic" terms as though the happiness he promises were not of this world (Wellmer, in Lara, 2003).

Considering this as a weak point in Adorno, Wellmer's attempt, on the contrary, is to place the aesthetic experience within the parameters of the world and does so through Habermas' theory of communicative action. The link that the paradigm of language and communication provides for the relations between one subject and another is a necessity. Mimesis, for Wellmer, is a kind of expressive rationality. Communication and intersubjectivity are therefore conditions for repositioning the role of aesthetics, not outside but within the world (*ibid.*: 82).

4. From simulacrum to performance

In recalling Hartog's regime of historicity, Perniola (2009) tells us that the present can be understood as a regime centred on communication. What characterizes this regime is that events escape rational explanation and have more the characteristics of "miracle and trauma". The space of multiple, elusive and contradictory events produces effects without historical actions, it exaggerates, falsifies, manipulates and mystifies reality. Communication then creates a product that occupies an intermediate space between the true and the false (*ibid.*).

To read contemporary communication in miraculous and traumatic terms leads Perniola to re-actualize simulacrum, as the aesthetic form chosen by individuals to survive in a media world. In the re-release, after thirty years, of the "society of simulacra" (2011), Perniola interprets simulacrum as a survival therapy, a mimesis to oppose the precariousness of existence, a way to transform demoralization into "an intoxication close to trance" (*ibid*: 8). He writes that simulacra are images and copies without the original "that impose their own effectiveness on the subject dissolving their reality" (Perniola 1980: 65). Simulacrum thus becomes the prevailing aesthetic for interpreting the way in which social actors, especially the youngest, inhabit the media environment.

Simulacrum is a paradoxical form of knowledge because, as Baudrillard (1981) tells us, through the mediation operated by the simulacrum, as the world is known, it is dissolved. Considering how media are inhabited, the reference to simulacrum is a *leitmotif*: not only in terms of common sense but, as the major literature recalls, a vertiginous dimension and hypnotic possession of the network. Simulacrum in its various meanings is a very seductive perspective full of charisma that has exercised a real interpretative dominion.

Why could performance, and not simulacrum, represent the aesthetic form pertinent to grasping the way in which subjects enter the

contemporary trans-media stream? Following Fry (2009)[3], simulacrum is indeed an acting out and therefore, to some extent, it introduces performance. Baudrillard's insistence that the crime of reality
is never "perfect" also means accepting the idea that between copy and
original, between reality and representation, there is still a gap (Baudrillard 1994; Savoldi 2016). A more in-depth reading of Baudrillard
shows how he absorbed the simulacrum of Klossowski, a version that
claims to have no nostalgia for the original.

Klossowsky writes that the driving depth cannot be expressed in
words, but in an instant of excitement: it is unintelligible (Klossowsky 1969). Emotion is by its nature unspeakable and incommunicable,
therefore the only relation with the real is made possible through re-
semblance; Klossowsky accepts the "end of representation" with en-
thusiasm and frees himself from feeling nostalgic (Cantarano, 1998:
181). Klossowsky's is a criticism of the institutional language that is the
supremacy of the word over experience. Simulacrum here is antago-
nistic to the language that imposes a fictitious identity.

In this version of Klossowsky's simulacrum, we find an anticipation of Butler's performance (2007) as a form of knowledge and as a
language of action on the world. For Butler, sexuality refers to a psychic excess evoked by the reference to the unconscious that cannot be
performed. Fry (2009)[4] says that for Butler "We perform identity, we
perform our subjectivity, we perform gender in all the ways but beyond
what we can perform, there is sexuality". Here performance, as something mysterious, surrounds sexuality as well as being, which cannot
be resolved or dissolved in the social.

Performative reflexivity could be characterized as an ambivalent
and 'situationist' response - in the sense of considering rationality as
a reactionary response - to the demand for high-performance in neoliberal societies. On one hand, it is consistent with the prescription
to be more and more innovative, creative and brilliant as required

3 https://oyc.yale.edu/english/engl-300/lecture-23
4 See footnote 3.

by the historical statement of the new spirit of capitalism (Boltansky and Chiappello 1999). On the other hand, it could mean the demand to legitimize psychic excess that can never be grasped or reduced by a prescription for performativity required by the labour market. Performance can represent a sort of acting-out to go beyond the paralysis of the contemporary moment.

5. Performance connectedness or performative connectivity?

Turner introduced the concept of performance in the social sciences in 1969. Alexander clarifies its meaning by explaining how performance is the way in which social actors "unfold in the eyes of others the meaning of their social action" (Alexander 2006: 32). In this definition Alexander delineates the preconditions for performance to succeed in some degree. It must convince an audience and succeed when all the elements are fused, when staging is credible and shareable and is able to conceal artifices. A successful performance has the same character as the collective ritual in traditional societies. It represents the social bond typical of the tribe founded on myth. Myth introduces the individual into a collective narrative that transcends him. Rather, medial performance more than community recalls connectedness.

In "Stati di connessione. Pubblici, cittadini, consumatori", Boccia Artieri (2012) writes about the reflexive practice exercised on the nature of relationships themselves. It is not content that determines communication but connection (*ibid.*: 55). What we observe is a state of potential and current connection that tends to naturalize, which cannot be simplified with the tautological reference to narcissism as a social pathology. We connect to share, participate, exhibit, differentiate, position ourselves in symbolic fields, etc., but the great number of connections changes the experience, because what changes is the "sense of position" in the world of communication (*ibid.*: 65).

Moreover, the experience changes because the criteria for reflection become connected; sharing becomes the value of social experience. What Boccia Artieri shows us is the connected process of hybridization between real and imagined lives, between mass media languages, advertising narratives and emotional experiences. What characterizes being in this hybrid and connected world? It is mainly and above all seen as tactile and bodily language; the staging of one's emotions is naturally channelled into an increasingly sensory reality. Here the media territory becomes an expressive space; people mix real and media territories, and narrate experiences recalling the body.

Whether "being connected" coincides with life in the pulsing of relationships, in the perspective of Simmel, here again we find the deep contradiction between life in its restless rhythm and the fixed duration of any particular form. Similarly to other publications[5], in "The Culture of Connectivity: A Critical History of Social Media", Van Dijck (2013) helps to understand the ambivalence of the contemporary digital–media scenario. Social media are online facilitators or enhancers of human networks, webs of people who promote connectedness as social value, individual ideas. Values and tastes are contagious and spread through human networks, but these networks also influence what individuals do and think (Christakis/Fowler 2009).

At the same time social media are automated systems that engineer and manipulate connections; for example, in order to recognize what people want and what they like, Facebook and other platforms track the source through coding relationships among people, things and ideas within algorithms. The meaning of social seems to encompass both human connectedness and automatic connectivity and its deliberate ambiguity. The technology-codified social network makes people's activities manageable and manipulable, engineering people's social life in daily routines.

5 Such as Mirko Schäfer's *Bastard culture! How user participation transforms cultural production* (2011) and Mark Deuze's *Media life* (2014).

Platforms based on detailed and intimate knowledge of people's desires and likes develop tools to create and manage specific needs, a button that shows what your friends watch, listen to and read, and the marketing recorders look at the tastes of your peers while at the same time configuring them. Users tend to emphasize human connection when they explain a value of the platform in their lives. Facebook helps its members to maintain contacts but there is an incontestable aspect of opacity: it is difficult to recognize how Facebook actively manages connections.

As Terranova explains (2016)[6], the Open Graph operating system underlying Facebook permits statistical data but also allows the reconstruction of maps of relationships. These dashboard data are kept well hidden in their database. Probably the administrator has access to these, but for example the researchers do not. Only once did they give permission to the social psychologists of Cornell University, who made an experiment of emotional contagion, an experiment to influence the emotions of 600,000 people that consisted of manipulating feeds, to see if emotional states could be transferred to others through emotional contagion.

This experiment remained little known because it would have opened a window on the total opacity of these platforms. Facebook or other platforms use their data for marketing purposes, and connectedness is often invoked for generated connectivity. So social, participation and collaboration, according to Van Dijck and Terranova, take on a new meaning. The ambivalence inherent in the dual concept of connectedness and connectivity remains unresolved and to some extent irreducible, proposing the Simmellian alternation between life and form in contemporary terms.

---

6 https://www.youtube.com/watch?v=eWnVLT7asUM

6. Life as art slips into the social

Paradoxical as it may appear, in observing trans-media collective storytelling, we witness the recovery of sensitivity or in other words the
direct presence of the body on the scene. The performative language
is a response to the discomfort of "being unseen", which is satisfied
with the visual (Abruzzese 2012). We are no longer just viewers but performers. In media performance, the subject appropriates something
that formerly adhered to art, which now moves into the social. There
seems to be a continuum between art and social. It is the social actors
who grasp the performer's gaze.

Performance as aesthetic reflexivity is intended to give potential to
action, underlines it, traces it and emphasizes it with the body. Performance in art anticipates and offers itself as a model in the evolution of
media languages. In the horizontal and uninterrupted flow of connections we find experiences of body art, happenings, experimentation.
The entire paradigm of art has shifted and the thinning of boundaries
and the confluences between art, technology and pop-media has widened the range of social performance.

With Duchamp we witness the passage from "representation
to presentation" (Di Giacomo, 2016: 73). This trend, from Duchamp
through pop art to minimalism, marks the possibility of giving form
to any objective content and finds the objective consistency of things
outside of every form. *Ready made* contains a self-reflexive dimension
because the object is used differently from everyday use and placed
to evoke an aesthetic contemplation. Can we also find this passage in
the social? *Have we all become a bit like Duchamp's readymades?* Perhaps
the attempt of individuals is not to form imaginary or utopian realities
that act as a stimulus to transformation but to constitute modes of existence or models of action within reality.

It is an art of life whose theoretical horizon is the sphere of human
relations. Perniola (2015) tries to grasp the dark side of this process: the
idea of expanding the field of art has become an imperative from which
it has proved impossible to escape. Indistinction between art and life

comes from the early twentieth century avant-gardes, which come to the point of presenting their self-denial and self-destruction as a qualitative leap compared to the conservation and repetition of the past. Since the 1960s all this has been exaggerated and radicalized beyond all limits, by the trend towards innovation and creativity amplified by mass media and subsequently digital communication. Assuming in itself the logic of journalism, fashion, advertising, marketing, technology and financial speculation, communication has created a global horizon in which becoming famous is worth much more than any other 'value'.

7. Exploration (not a conclusion)

In this chapter we have introduced how the social actor uses media grammars, imagining this reflection as a necessary premise for the cultural planning of innovative spaces. The artwork enters the space through social actors. What we refer to is not a matter of *art* but of a tension that makes one's life a work of art, a radicalization of the spirit of aesthetics and Oscar Wilde at the beginning of last century. The new territories are above all playgrounds in which virtual and real, control and loss of control, fiction and contingency communicate and overlap.

Social performers today combine communication strategies: pieces of poetry, songs, body performances, moments of everyday life, improvisations putting within their own story the words of others or friends or family, imaginary scenes or even pieces of literary work. With all these artefacts they build the self, create a storytelling where there is an affirmation, a claim to affirm that particular lives are important.

If the explorations of this chapter are plausible then social space becomes a dynamic installation to provide social actors with the possibility to interject something that seems to them relevant or legitimate. The intervention by a user is integrated into a hypertext that is not only more extensive but substantially unpredictable in its future developments and in its overall configuration. Social space rises even more from this interactive and deeply shared process.

References

Abruzzese, A. (2001): L'Intelligenza del Mondo, Fondamenti di Storia e Teoria dell'Immaginario, Roma: Meltemi.
Abruzzese, A. (2012): La Bellezza per Me e per Te. Saggi contro l'Estetica, Napoli: Liguori.
Adorno, T.W. (1975): Teoria estetica, Torino: Einaudi.
Alexander, J. (2006): Social Performance: Symbolic Action, Cultural Pragmatics and Ritual, Cambridge: Cambridge University Press.
Baudrillard, J. (1981): Simulacres et Simulation, Paris: Galilée.
Beck, U./Giddens, A./Lash, S. (1994): Reflexive Modernization: Politics, Tradition and Aesthetics in the Modern Social Order, Stanford: Stanford University Press.
Boccia Artieri, G. (2004): I Media-Mondo: Forme e Linguaggi dell'Esperienza Contemporanea, Milano: Meltemi.
Boccia Artieri, G. (2012): Stati di Connessione: Pubblici, Cittadini e Consumatori nella (Social) Network Society, Milano: Franco Angeli.
Boltanski, L./Chiappello, E. (1999): Le Nouvel Esprit du Capitalisme, Paris: Gallimard.
Buck-Morss, S. (1992): "Aesthetics and Anaesthetics: Walter Benjamin's Artwork Essay Reconsidered": October/62, pp. 3-41.
Butler, J. (2007): Gender Troubles. Feminism and the Subversion of Identity, London: Routlledge.
Canevacci, M. (2007): Una Stupita Fatticità. Feticismi Visuali tra Corpi e Metropoli, Milano: Costa & Nolan.
Cantarano, G. (1998): Immagini del Nulla: la Filosofia Italiana Contemporanea, Milano: Pearson Italia.
Christakis, N./Folwer, J. (2009): Connected: The Amazing Power of Social Networks and How They Shape Our Lives, London: Harper Press.

D'Andrea, F./Federici, M.C. (2004): Lo Sguardo Obliquo: Dettagli e Totalità nel Pensiero di George Simmel, Perugia: Morlacchi.

Debord, G. (1967): La Société du Spectacle, Paris: Buchet-Chastel.

Deuze, M. (2012): Media Life, Cambridge: Polity Press.

Di Giacomo, G. (2016): Arte e Modernità. Una Guida Filosofica, Roma: Carocci.

Fry, P. (2009): "Introduction to Theory of Literature" September 1st, (https://www.youtube.com/watch?v=4YY4CTSQ8nY).

Gemini, L. (2003): L' Incertezza Creativa: i Percorsi Sociali e Comunicativi delle Performance Artistiche, Milano: Franco Angeli.

Hartog, F. (2002): Regime d'Historicité. Présentisme et Expériences du temps, Paris: Seuil.

Klossowsky, P. (1969): Nietzsche et le Cercle Vicieux, Paris: Mercure de France.

Korom, F.J. (2013): The Anthropology of Performance: A Reader, Hoboken NJ: Wiley-Blackwell.

Lara, M.P. (2003): Intrecci Morali. Narrazioni Femministe della Sfera Pubblica, Roma: Armando Editori.

Lash, S. (1999): Another Modernity, a Different Rationality, Hoboken NJ: John Wiley & Sons.

Latour, B. (2005): Reassembling the Social: an Introduction to Actor-Network-Theory, Oxford: Oxford University Press.

Martucelli, D. (2010): La Société Singulariste, Paris: Armand Colin.

McLuhan, M. (1962): The Gutenberg Galaxy. The Making of Typographic Man, Toronto: University of Toronto Press.

Perniola, M. (2009): Miracoli e Traumi della Comunicazione, Torino: Einaudi.

Perniola, M. (1980): La Società dei Simulacri, Bologna: Cappelli.

Perniola, M. (2011): "La Società dei Simulacri", in Agalma 20-21, pp. 7-20.

Perniola, M., (2015): L'Arte Espansa, Torino: Einaudi.

Savoldi, G. (2016): (https://www.azioniparallele.it/30-eventi/atti,-contributi/125-pensare-radicalmente-il-reale.htmll).

Schäfer, M.T. (2011): Bastard Culture!: How User Participation Transforms Cultural Production, Amsterdam: Amsterdam University Press.

Simmel, G./Frisby, D/ Featherstone, M. (1997, eds.): Simmel on Culture: Selected Writings, London: Sage.

St John, G. (2008): Victor Turner and Contemporary Cultural Performance, New York and Oxford: Berghahn Books.

Tavani, E. (2013): L'Immagine e la Mimesis. Arte, Tecnica, Estetica in Theodor W. Adorno, Pisa: Edizioni ETS.

Terranova, T. (2004): Network Culture: Politics for the Information Age, London: Pluto Press.

Terranova, T. (2016), Workshop on "Soggettivazione e Assoggettamento nel Cyberspazio" (https://www.youtube.com/watch?v=eWnVL-T7asUM), Milano: Università Bicocca.

Van Dijck, J. (2013): The Culture of Connectivity: A Critical History of Social Media, New York: Oxford University Press.

Wellmer, A. (2015): The Persistence of Modernity: Aesthetics, Ethics and Postmodernism, Hoboken New Jersey: John Wiley & Sons.

Wulf, C. (1995): Mimesis l'Arte e i suoi Modelli, Milano: Mimesis.

Žižek, S. (1997): The Plague of Fantasies, London: Verso.

Žižek, S. (1997): Premio Hemingway, 2017 (http://www.filosofia.rai.it/articoli/žižek-il-rapporto-tra-lo-schermo-e-la-realtà/37954/default.aspx).

DEACCESSIONING AND RE-LOCATING
NEW OPTIONS FOR MUSEUMS

Federica Antonucci

1. Enhancing cultural heritage might be a tricky challenge

Cultural heritage is a complex and multi-faceted topic which one of the most controversial debates of the contemporary scenario is focused upon. In the art system, but more in general in society, museums have been identified as the vehicle of art valorization with specific and established duties. There is a general sense that conceive cultural heritage preservation as the museum's *raison d'être*, in order to keep the memory of human testimony alive. Indeed, it is undeniable that its own main and primary function is to hand down this inheritance. Talking about enhancement might be very tricky, in fact through the years it has passed across many different definitions and categories, initially even considered evanescent and fleeting concept. During the 1960s, a first interpretation was given in terms of activities aiming at the promotion, the enjoyment and the diffusion of cultural heritage but it was still kept separated from the conservation duties. Moreover, Italy had waited until 2001 to see enhancement regulation codified in the art. 117 of the Italian Constitution (Antonucci, 2016).

Why enhancing heritage is so important? Basically, the answer is quite easy: it might be stated that the bent to show and enhance cultural heritage is always teetering between the potentiality to express the actual value of cultural goods and the managing criteria under-

taken by cultural institutions[1]. As a consequence, it makes sense to
talk about cultural enhancement as a relevant artistic, economic and
social growth element. In this chapter I will try to figure out different
solutions adopted by museums in their own collection's management
system, bearing in mind the mandatory and essential goal of pursuing
public interest[2] (Casini, 2016).

To sustain the primary and final museums' objective – that is usually identified with the collection's enhancement – museums need
solid financial measures at disposal (Sanesi, 2018). Nowadays, many
cultural institutions have to deal with burdensome economic issues
risking to entail the devolpment of normal activities; on the one hand,
public museums continuously deal with a gradual reduction of public
funds, on the other hand even the most well-known private organizations are not able to survive by their own resources in spite of public
accountability, qualitative fundraising and self-managing ability, as
the pre-bankruptcy crisis of the Metropolitan Museum of New York
(Mattiacci, 2008) shows.

Almost in the last thirty years, cultural policies have been changed,
embodying a wider range of citizens' and the so called cultural consumers' flavours and needs. "Consuming art" has increasingly become
a harder social demand to please on the part of cultural policies: people
ask for spectacular initiatives, such as new museums openings, innovative art collections' exhibitions, important artworks' restorations

---

1 Museums to carry out their activities have to carefully balance their duties, caring
oh the one hand about preserving, enhancing its own belongings but on the other
hand to have to be financially sustainable avoiding the risk of bankruptcy.

2 Existing copyright laws have traditionally attempted to define public interest as
strictly related to Cultural Heritage, for example: J.H. Merryman splits public interest in four elements: preservation, cultural truth, public accessibility and cultural
nationalism; Jayme in *Globalization in Art Law*, uses to divide it in five different categories: as a globally society interest (considering also accessibility and movements
of goods for exhibition purposes), the capacity of Public policies to preserve cultural good with a relevant national value, artists and owners' private interests, good
preservation' interests and market interests.

and each time different, curious, rare and stimulating temporary exhibitions to visit.

2. What are museums made of?

Big exhibition rooms, transparent crates hosting precious and delicate artworks, captivating light beams illuminating breath-taking paintings, some isolated chairs where tired visitors can rest and probably a healing cafeteria and a bookshop. Actually, what is described above is just what people see and live into the museum, but there is another part, hidden and out of consumption that should be considered as the institution's beating heart. It is deposits.

Many museums, both in Italy and abroad, keep a significant part of their collections locked in storage and, in recent years, the desire not just to show the objects in the best possible way but also to open the doors and allow people to come into contact with unknown spaces and artworks, has become increasingly evident.

It is a long time that the debate between preservation and enhancement of cultural goods is going on; on the one hand, indeed, a conservation-oriented vision is afraid about a possible unscrupulous use of cultural heritage and fights to keep it safe; on the other hand, at the opposite, a market-oriented wing thinks that enhancing that heritage should be considered a fundamental economic asset (Donato, 2010), able to tackle the dilemma of cultural heritage profitability troubles.

The enhancement argument, that has involved the whole cultural system for several years and is still heated, with the growing importance of cultural economic discipline made almost real by the Italian 'legge Ronchey' in 1993 (aimed at combining public and private provision of services in state museums), has changed directions. In fact, the focus was shifted on the privatization of public services into the museums' scenario and the introduction of some economic profit-oriented measures.

Actually, the enhancement *ratio* was totally different. Cultural heritage needed to be part of a change and even if its preservation is an unassailable value, it cannot be conceived as a passive action aimed at mere conservation. Opting out of caring about cultural goods sustainability in favour of a static conservative dynamic could run the risk of neglecting their value and moreover denying their shared enjoyment. Finally, the real challenge is to devise a combined system able to merge both sides, in order to implement an active form of preservation of our heritage.

Precisely, the commitment of promoting and divulgating cultural heritage, especially as a common good, and actions aimed to protect and enhance it must be underpinned in the interests of stimulating public and citizens' participation. And in so doing, paradoxically thanks to the proper use of cultural resources, it becomes possible to guarantee their preservation. To conclude, considering the neverending transformation of contemporary society it is crucial to ask ourselves: which contribution do we want to produce on people's quality of life through cultural policies? Are museums able to generate any kind of cultural and social impact? The answer is undeniably affirmative.

Due to the fundamental role of museums and cultural institutions in general, even according to the ICOM (2010) definition, we must acknowledge that their social function has to be maintained, contributing to the promotion and the devolpment of culture. Now, after having defined the general framework, the scenario looks focused on some major troubles. First of all, keeping artworks closed into museums' deposits may sound as a vital and necessary obligation to be adopted, but the extremely conservative vision shared by many museum professionals makes them blind to a more versatile evidence. Indeed, deposits generate a huge cost in which museums incur; not only a financial cost but mostly the cost – borne by society – of limited enjoyment, education, cultural growth and, from museums' perspective, of a very limited opportunity to establish an efficient exhibition system turnover among institutions, denying the chance to show what is often hidden and out of consumption.

3. New experiences in the contemporary scenario

"Museums, like many other heritage attractions, are essentially experiential products, quite literally constructions to facilitate experience.
In this sense, museums are about facilitating feelings and knowledge
based upon personal observation or contact by their visitors" (Prentice,
1996).

Museums need to tackle five traditional duties: to collect, to preserve, to study, to exhibit, and to interpret objects of their own collection (ICOM, 2013). Carrying out their mission, museums deal with several activities: they acquire objects either by donation or purchase and
thus take care of their collections by monitoring them; museums produce research through the work of in-house curators or making their
collection available to academics and professionals. Certainly, museums produce exhibitions allowing the audience to enjoy their own permanent and temporary collections. Moreover, they play the vital role of
educating the audience through exhibitions and specific services.

Art museums' crucial assets are their permanent collections. In
fact, these are the key resources museums manage as they fulfil their
public mandate. The collection is the very heart of a museum and since
all the activities undertaken depend on the collection, then artworks
preservation is paramount (Stebbins, 1991). If artworks are denied to
audience visibility, not useful for research purposes, and not needing
any specific restoration actions at the moment, their very reason for
being in a museum is almost murky: "Museum's objects are not the
mission of the museum's work but powerful tools that enable it" (Skramstad, 1997).

Thus, to try to keep as many artworks as possible accessible appears
to be the right direction to chase. In recent times, maybe the most important museum of the entire world, the Louvre, has decided to open
another Louvre venue in Liévin, just next to the older structure built
in Lens. Another challenge has been mounted by the Museum, after
the birth of Abu Dhabi Louvre and the Lens one, in fact the project's
aim is to create a new space able to host the big number of objects that

nowadays are located into the stocks. Through the decades the Louvre Museum has collected huge reserves of artworks thanks to extensive acquisition policies, but it is also true that being so close to the Seine river could endanger them.

After a past similar episode which forced the museum to close for some days in order to repair the damages, the directorate took the decision to create a specific-dedicated site where the stocks could be protected and preserved. The new Louvre in Liévin was born as a conservation center where more than 200.000 artworks are going to be kept. The promising project will be inaugurated in 2019 and the new conservation center could pave the way to a new idea of museum, where the background restoration works could be showed live to the visitors who can have the chance, for the very first time, to join and share a completely unusual visit experience[3].

4. Concluding remarks

"Museums are doing amazingly well, but can they keep the visitors coming?" (The Economist, 2013). The cultural market, just like every other market, deals with demand and supply, exchanging art, music, performing arts, literature and more in general all the initiatives, sensations, patterns, tools to ingenerate knowledge, emotional and intellectual fulfillment. "Doing culture" is such a hard duty, but first we have to start asking ourselves which is the real meaning of culture.

---

3 In 2012, the Louvre directorate decided to open a third venue, beside the main one in Paris and the other one in Abu Dhabi, in Lens. Lens is in the mining region of Nord-Pas de Calais, and after being hard bitted by the economic crisis, it was decided to give a re-born chance to the city led by cultural policies. The new Lens Louvre has become not only the iconic symbol of the new contemporary architecture but also a virtuous space able to host many artworks from the main venue with the aim of mobilize the collections' heritage and make it more visible. Indeed, Louvre of Lens can be defined as "museum *in fieri*" because the 20% of its collection is renovated each year and at least every five years the exhibition changes.

If on the hand the question is whether or not in cultural production an audience is a *conditio sine qua non*, on the other hand there is another school of thought that doesn't accept the need of this requirement to be recognized as culture[4].

We might say that even if the audience requirement is not necessary, it is also true that museums and cultural institutions more in general produce exhibitions to be enjoyed by visitors: without them their work would be unnecessary. In this scenario, considering the upcoming technological innovations, the chance to have an on-line museum visit, museums should consider the option of becoming more appealing and attractive to maintain their role.

Museums are not really future-oriented, but it might exist a way to be innovative with respect to their collections and their existing mission. Broadening the lending activities to increase the artworks turnover in museums, including also minor museums into successful networks; wondering to expose copies of hidden and precious artworks and avoiding risks of damages, pursuing a wider diffusion of art objects in order for people to be encouraged to visit them. At least an extreme solution, when possible, would be to sell objects: some of the major museums, such as Prado, keep over 90 per cent of their endowment locked in their deposits: these artworks are never showed to the public.

A reasonable selling system could allow museums to lighten their stock with the less prominent pieces in order for them to raise funds aimed at acquiring more consistent objects for a more appropriate interpretation of their collections; the sold artworks may add value to other minor museum's collections (Rizzo and Towse, 2016). Even if

---

4 The Arts, more generally speaking, are something somewhere between hedonism and entrainment (Pellegrini, 2016). Since ancient times, starting from the Greece concept of Paideia to the Eighties social gathering, Culture wasn't conceived as a shared value, but something that belonged to the few. Concomitantly to the Industrial Revolution, to the renewed role of working class, to the feminism and the student's movement, it becomes increasingly clear that culture is democratic value, accessible to everyone.

museums tend to be stuck in an unmovable condition, with the recent cultural changes something has started to change, paving the way for a new creative direction to be followed in the years that lay ahead.

References

Antonucci, F. (2016): La gestione delle collezioni museali: strategie, politiche e impatto, Roma: EAI.

Casini, L. (2016). Ereditare il futuro. Dilemmi sul patrimonio culturale, Bologna: Il Mulino.

Desvallèes, A./Mairesse, F. (2010), Key Concepts of Museology. Paris: ICOM.

Donato, F./Visser Travagli, A. (2010): Il muro oltre la crisi. Dialogo fra museologia e management. Milano: Electa.

The Economist (2013): Museums. Temples of delight, special report, December 21st.

ICOM (2013): Code of ethics for Museums, Paris: internal report.

Il giornale delle fondazioni (2018): Musei, bilancio di sostenibilità e dintorni (http://www.bing.com/cr?IG=53E87E7CA03548F89CD5 8D35BC148EDE&CID=1861F55802D46D250EFAFED8037B6C3E& rd=1&h=axXUSkqty1aWEf91iDioZmMPFQg1S9JWWNWbcW RaWQQ&v=1&r=http%3a%2f%2fwww.ilgiornaledellefondazioni. com%2fcontent%2fmusei-bilancio-di-sostenibilit%25C3%25A0-e-dintorni&p=DevEx,5065.1), special report, January 23rd.

Mattiacci, A. (2008): La gestione dei beni artistici e culturali nell'ottica del Mercato, Milano: Guerini e Associati.

Pellegini, D. (2016): "Fare cultura attraverso la complessità", Che-fare. https://www.che-fare.com/cultura-complessita/, June 21st.

Prentice, R. (1996): "Managing implosion: The facilitation of insight through the provision of context", Museum Management and Curatorship, 15/2, pp. 169-185.

Rizzo, I./Towse, R. (2016, eds.): The Artful Economist, Zurich: Springer.

Sanesi, I. (2016): Museo quo vadis?, Il Giornale delle Fondazioni, June 20ᵗʰ.

Site officiel du musée du Louvre-Lens - Un lieu de découverte et d'émerveillement. 2018. Louvre-Lens. https://www.louvrelens.fr, January 23, 2018.

Skramstad, H. (1997): Changing Public Expectations of Museums, Museums for the New Millennium. Washington, D.C.: Center for Museum Studies, Smithsonian Institution and the American Association of Museums.

Stebbins, T.E. (1991): The Museum' s Collection, in Feldstein, M. (ed.) The Economics of Art Museums, Chicago: The University of Chicago Press.

PUBLIC SPACE AND ITS CHALLENGES
A PALIMPSEST FOR URBAN COMMONS

Lidia Errante

1. Foreword

In future cities we will have to deal with challenges of different sorts related to the irreversible overpopulation of urban citizens, which the UN estimates will reach 6.5 billion in 2030. "The population problem has no technical solution; it requires a fundamental extension in morality" assert Garret Hardin in his paper about *The Tragedy of the Commons* (Hardin, 1968): population is growing exponentially, consuming a prodigious amount of energy enough to jeopardize the very concept of common goods. Because of these circumstances, the international debate is now oriented around issues like holistic sustainability, quality of life, well-being and urban happiness in the built environment, in order to reverse this point of view.

At the same time, the "recent revival of emphasis upon the supposed loss of urban commonalities reflects the seemingly profound impacts of the recent wave of privatizations, enclosures, spatial controls, policing and surveillance upon the qualities of urban life [...] and the potentiality to build or inhibit new forms of social relations" (Harvey, 2012: 67). Public space has a transversal role in the whole discussion, crossing each of these issues and ensuring the delicate balance between the physical and the social domains of the city. As observed by Stephen Carr (1992: 3) in his very accurate definition of public space, it is "the stage upon which the drama of communal life unfolds".

From this perspective, the *publicness* of public space is enhanced by the presence of life that is communal, collective, and shared between individuals that are simultaneously the actors and the audience of this 'drama'. In such a respect, discussing the quality of urban life seems to be a wide and democratic issue, since we live almost all in built environments and are joined by the same interests in political and cultural debates about the places we live in, regardless of age or social background.

In terms of political efforts, research and literature production, the social role of public space, and of urban design too, has been reconsidered in the public agendas as the proper tool to be adopted for a better quality of urban life. In both material and immaterial ways public space is crafted by how it is lived, by the criss-crossing flows around, inside and outside the built domain during the many everyday-life activities. This phenomenon has remained unchanged throughout the centuries, even if it has been weakened or neglected by social, political and economic forces that have altered the sense of living the city.

2. What challenges for the cities?

In the last century urban forms and ideals have left us a tangible testimony of the fracture that occurred between the social shaping of the city and the rational, functional and capitalist one, and it acts as a clue of what can happen when people are left out of the urban scale in terms of habits, activities, mobility, and proportions. The functionalist approach to space, especially in the suburbs, has been dramatically conditioned by the rules of free market (Bottini, 2010: 16).

Cities have been transformed by way of highways and automobiles in order to let people spread and circulate all over a territory, superimposing a traffic infrastructure over a socio-spatial one, regardless of what they spread across or at what cost. This kind of approach has determined a fragmentation of public space as a whole, seriously affecting pedestrian mobility, accessibility and interfering with the many social, cultural and recreational activities of everyday life[1] (De Certeau, 1984), related to the processes of territorialization (Madanipour, 2003) and the different practices that transform space into places (Nor-berg-Schultz, 1979). Moreover, the tendency to attribute specific functions to urban spaces has led to an additional social fragmentation in which people are labelled in formal categories (Sebastiani, 2010: 238-239), "destroying the integrity of the individuals, isolating them from society and depriving them of any defence" (De Carlo, 2013: 66).

On one hand the disconnection between the two key elements of urban dynamics – a society/space – has impacted upon the decline of public space, worsened by political inability to deal with the issue and the growing privatization of entire urban areas. On the other hand, urban design and public space have gained more importance and presence in public agendas and, what is more, there has been an increasing awareness that a well-designed public space can improve and enhance the social life it contains, positively affecting people's perceptions and users' activities. As Jan Gehl observes, "first we shape the cities – then they shape us" (Gehl, 2013). In this respect it has been recognized that there is a need for new and sharper tools to identify and analyze problems and develop specific solutions, in order to navigate the rising number of variables existing in such an inter-disciplinary framework. More importantly, it requires the ability to address also large-scale problems in the inter-scalar dimension of public space, in order to understand phenomena in each particular and general feature of city space and city life.

As Micheal Sandel argues[2], market solutions applied to the city cannot work on the immaterial domains of civil life and social practices: markets do not care about values and intrinsic meanings. What the market system has corrupted is indeed communality, civic en-

---

1 Identified by De Certeau as talking, walking, shopping, staying, playing (1984).
2 Michael Sandel during the TED Conference in Edinburgh, 2013: https://www.ted.com/talks/michael_sandel_why_we_shouldn_t_trust_markets_with_our_civ-ic_life?language=it

gagement, social practices and the chance to recognize that "we are all in this together". For these reasons the concept of the 'right to the city' suggested by Henri Lefebvre (1974) has been used as a motto for whoever is trying to survive this era of privatization and neoliberal development of cities, adapting the way in which responsibilities are conceived.

In such a respect local bodies are the ones who have granted market economy to invest in speculations, tourism facilities and housing estates over public spaces. On the other hand, the community is the one who wants back the chance to define the rules in the neighbourhood, in terms of relations between individuals and the governance of the common ground, in order to live in a nicer and open place. Continuing along the path offered by Lefebvre, we can use his "Spatial Triad" to identify the main themes of urban space. The social production of space, as previously said, strictly depends on the collaborative interrelations of many dimension, which the author identifies as conceived, perceived and lived space. Each dimension represents a scale, a way to shape space, its specific tools and the actors able to use them.

The representations of space – or how it is conceived – refers to how it is actually used as a bi-dimensional or tri-dimensional medium by professionals and planners. Spatial practice is related to how space is perceived through its design, and representational space is how the space is lived and used by the inhabitants, including cultural and intangible elements. Moving the discussion to the level of the social actors involved, we can rightfully assume that the production of space can be better explained as the result of a combination of choices made by planners, designers and users, who, of course, could affect one another.

Taking into account how the tangible and intangible fragmentation of public space infrastructure has affected the quality of urban life, it seems plausible to consider the process of *commoning* as a virtuous trigger, able to catalyze creative energies – hopefully positive and proactive – in the transformation of an area. Even if the *commoning* process appears unclear, it seems to be a potentially achievable and

hopefully the right approach to holistic sustainability – social, economic and environmental – as well as a strong alternative to the contemporary urban models in which we are living. Nonetheless, *urban
commons* and urban design seems to be a good combination.

In order to provide us with a framework, commons can be defined
(Ostrom, 1990) as those communal goods and services whose property
is not referable neither to public authority nor to private corporations,
and can be identified on the basis of three elements: the common or
collective property; the *commoning* attribute, as something depending
on human decisions and activities; the autonomy from market or state
forms of management. In this respect a common is an object of collaboration, an activity carried out by people and a form of management
and ownership (David Bollier, 2014).

As argued by David Harvey, one of the issue in commons is the
scale problem, which is clearer as we jump from one scale to another,
when the nature of the problems and the prospects of finding a solution change dramatically (2012: 69). As far as we can say, several studies
have demonstrated that at the city scale the governance of the urban
commons (Ostrom, 1990) can succeed only taking into account why
and in what circumstances the *commoning process* works or not, and in
particular in what combination of public and private instrumentalities,
underlying of course the need of some kind of "hierarchical form" of
organization (*ibid.*).

In terms of planning and its ethical mission on the themes of quality of urban life and welfare state, this hierarchy became clearer after
the Second World War, translated as a quantitative tool to support and
rationalize the new phase of development, production, reconstruction and income redistribution (Bottini, 2010: 15). More recently, the
discussion has been oriented on the quality of public space and closely related to other and more specific urban issues, like sustainability,
land consumption, global warming, health, urban happiness. In this
interdisciplinary perspective, which has also been embraced by several
less recent authors like Jan Gehl or Jane Jacobs, attention is paid to how
public space can affect other fields of investigation, recognizing the

potential outcomes of social and spatial metabolism in cities (Bottini, 2010: 13).

Through this lens many authors argue that the quality and the decay of public space share the same roots. In general terms, it is reasonable to believe that the decay of urban public spaces is strictly related to the practices of abstraction allowed by public policies and carried out through planning (Sebastiani, 2010: 238). More specifically, Matthew Carmona has identified several elements which have compromised the quality of urban spaces in the fields of privatization, commodification, maintenance and accessibility. Moreover, he suggests that maintenance is the key to determining the success of public space in terms of liveability and users' perceptions. Even if this could resemble a cliché or perhaps common sense, this position shifts the whole discourse on public space performance in terms of how public and/or private bodies carry out their roles.

Again, the *commoning process* aims to solve this rough dialogue between the two sides of the coin, offering alternative approaches and methodologies to the challenges of public space. Design, urban furniture or formal categories cannot be considered anymore as quality indicators, even if such equipment can increase and enhance – or even decrease – the way space is used and lived by people. What public space needs today is to be responsive, well-maintained, organised, diversified and controlled by and for the urban community in order to be a place of the people.

Inevitably, the non-planned interstitial areas of the city became object of increasing interest, both from local authorities and from civil society, as blank space ready to be transformed into liveable urban spaces. Local bodies recognize the strategic value in urban regeneration processes that are aimed at achieving quality and sustainability goals. Community – meaning private and individual subjects, associations and/or social cooperatives – has sometimes filled the institutional gap in the management of public space through its informal occupation, sometimes unauthorized, in order to offer an alternative and civil use of forgotten places of the city. These kinds of soft transformation initiatives have positively affected the social perception of marginalized areas, reopening the debate on new ways of public-private partnerships and place-making.

On the other hand, the concept of *urban commons* is more frequently used to explore solution in terms of "new or alternative collaborative (and co-management) arrangements between city administrators, 'active' citizens, and private property owners for managing certain kinds of space within the urban area); this signifies a paradigm shift from a very formal way of conceiving space to a communal, collective or simply human way of designing it, involving people in the decision-making as equal stakeholders to any other professionals or investors". Of course, an effort is needed to push the limits of public-private and state-market dichotomies (Harvey, 2012: 69) and means-purposes, in which *informal commoning* and processes do not find a specific location.

The very same social practices that produce public space can be transformed into policies, though not necessarily by political parties or institutions, filling the gap between the social and the territorial meaning, as well as Giancarlo De Carlo has done developing his own process of participating architecture. More particularly, from an institutional point of view it seems reasonable to ask public bodies to deal with public space in order to avoid those obstacles that could jeopardize the socio-spatial dynamics at the basis of its production, rather than worrying about how to create new spaces (Sebastiani, 2010: 239-240).

Quoting Giancarlo De Carlo and his considerable relevance in the contemporary scenario, "the problem of *why* is now prevailing on the problem of *how*". At the same time, talking about participation but legitimately referring the whole discourse on the commoning process, a change of direction from *how* to *why* is possible by doing and experimenting certain tactics (De Carlo, 2013: 66-68). Moreover, the idea of co-city as an urban form built in the age of collaboration also reclaims the Lefebvrian vision of urban as a complex, adaptive and evolutionary system rather than a fixed space (Foster & Iaione, 2016: 84-85) and the participation process, in which the architectural form – or the urban form in this case – has to deal with the perception and the demand of self-expression of the users (De Carlo, 2013: 70-71).

As Sofia Mazzuco states regarding urban commons and public space, there are four elements that must be taken into account: repurposed public spaces, collective governance, hands-on action and resulting benefits that support community and urban development in terms of social, economic and environmental aspects. Of course, the open and spontaneous collective appropriation and repurposing of public spaces needs to be structured in order to be effective and to guarantee those benefits for the community, strengthen a collaborative development model and contribute to the "awareness of the city as networked spaces, people and resources that mutually impact each other".

The social construction of space should be rightfully replaced and enhanced by the *commoning* process, equally able to address both spatial and social quality goals. In fact, the common is a social practice, constructed "as an unstable and malleable social relation between a particular self-defined social group and those aspects of its actually existing or yet-to-be-created social and/or physical environment deemed crucial to its life and livelihood". On the other hand, even if this social production cannot be destroyed, of course it can be banalized by its abuse, as it happens when a street is crowded by automobiles and requires interventions in order to restore its primal balance of civilization (Harvey, 2012: 73-74). Through this lens, it becomes easy to look at public space as a socio-spatial infrastructure and at the same time notice a general lack of tools to define and shape roles and responsibilities, distribute them to different actors included in those kind of processes, and clarify a specific planning model.

The strategic value of the *commoning* processes has been widely acknowledged in Italy as well, where it has been approved as the first regulation on urban commons in 2014 by the municipality of Bologna. The Italian Pavilion at the *XV La Biennale di Architettura di Venezia* bears witness to a renewed interest in a "concrete vision of an architecture at the service of the community [...] that makes the difference taking care of individuals and communities, of spaces and places" (Galloni in TAM Associati, 2016: 12). At the same time, quoting Paolo Baratta, the President of *La Biennale di Venezia*, "The majority [of the authorities in charge of governance and spatial planning, especially local authorities, with very tighter budgets] rather than governing development and investing incomings, try to fill their accounts seeking funds in the spontaneous development and in the revenues they can obtain in exchange for concessions" (Baratta in TAM Associati, 2016: 10-11). Indeed, the *commoning* process is often influenced by informal experiences and associations that drive urban experimentation and change. In practice, urban commons are a social and territorial laboratory: the ground for innovation in the architecture, planning and urban design fields in which interested professionals and citizens can share opinions and visions, participating and deciding together on a common aim.

One of many examples is Farm Cultural Park in Favara[3], Agrigento, a small town that has been almost unknown until the opening of the cultural center. Founded and promoted by a private couple (wife and husband), this cultural institution has revealed how a *commoning* process can be seen as an urban acupuncture action, with specific purposes and a wide range of sustainable outcomes. Starting from a very low budget and quick transformations in the so called 'seven courtyards', Farm Cultural Park has actually changed its decayed face scarred with illegal buildings by combining urban regeneration and social values, changing Favara's perception amongst both inhabitants and outsiders. So far, Farm Cultural Park has invested twenty million euros to create opportunities, attract talented artists and performers, open a school of architecture for children and become a contemporary art destination within the established cultural heritage network in the area.

---

3 All the information on Farm Cultural Park are taken from TAM Associati (Ed.). (2016). *Taking Care: progettare per il bene comune – Catalogo Padiglione Italia de La Biennale di Venezia, XV Mostra internazionale di Architettura.* Padova, Italia: Becco Giallo.

3. Conclusions

Of course, the discussion on urban commons and in general on the process of commoning has to deal with the contradictions arising from the impact of such interventions on the territory, which sometimes might actually decrease rather than enhance the benefits for the inhabitants. More specifically, we can refer to the property values or rents, often increased by the creation of such public spaces, as it happened for the High Line of New York, which has denied access to affordable housing in the nearby area (Harvey, 2012: 75). Other critical aspects are represented by the difficulties in the dialogue between the different actors involved – basically identified as the city itself, the entrepreneurs, the social partners, the knowledge institutes and the social innovators – which is problematic almost everywhere. The case of Farm Cultural Park is not an exception: regardless of the international prestige of artists and architects involved in the design of the temporary pavilions placed in the courtyards, the Mayor of Favara has disposed their immediate removal – judging their presence as illegal – only to waive the requirement a couple of weeks later. The episode had such an impact on public opinion that the petition *We are Farm Cultural Park*[4] has gained six thousand signatures in two days in order to prevent the removal of the artworks.

All these arguments on public space and the *commoning process* eventually confirm the idea of a social-spatial infrastructure, in which tangible and intangible elements, dimensions and actors play their role individually, cross-fertilizing each other at the same time. All the energies provided by the circulation flow and the many everyday-life activities in public space can be catalyzed in the process of creating urban commons and catabolized into proactive and creative forces, able to drive a change in the way we conceive, use and take care of public space. In this respect, the infrastructure of public space can be used

---

4 More information at: https://www.change.org/p/noi-siamo-farm-cultural-park

as an urban *palimpsest* in which the tale of the co-city can finally be overwritten.

References

Augé, M. (1992). *Non-Lieux, introduction à une anthropologie de la surmodernité.* Paris: Le Seuil.

Balbo, M. (2015). *Migrazioni e piccoli comuni.* Milano: FrancoAngeli.

Bollier, D. (2014). *Think Like a Commoner: A Short Introduction to the Life of the Commons.* New Society Publishers .

Bottini, F. (2010). Questo libro: perché. In F. Bottini, *Spazio Pubblico – Declino, Difesa, Riconquista* (pp. 13-17). Roma: Eddiesse.

Briata, P. (2014). *Spazio urbano e immigrazione in Italia Esperienze di pianificazione in una prospettiva europea.* Milano: FrancoAngeli.

Cancellieri, A. (2012). *Tracce Urbane Alla ricerca della città .* Milano : FrancoAngeli .

Carmona, M. (2010). Contemporary Public Space, Part Two: Classification. *Journal of Urban Design* (15), 157-173.

Carmona, M. (2010). Contemporary Public Space: Critique and Classification, Part One: Critique. *Journal of Urban Design , 15*, 123-148.

Carr, S. e. (1992). *Public Space.* New York, US: Cambridge University Press.

Council of Europe Ministers of Foreign Affairs. (June, 2008). *White Paper on Intercultural Dialogue "Living Together As Equals in Dignity".* F-67075 Strasbourg Cedex, Strasbourg.

Croso Mazzuco, S. (2017, July 28). From LabGov – Laboratory for the Governance of the City as a Commons: http://www.labgov.it/2017/07/28/public-space-collective-governance-and-the-urban-commons/

De Carlo, G. (2015). *L'architettura della partecipazione .* (S. Marini, Ed.) Macerata: Quodlibet.

De Carlo, G. (2013). *L'architettura della partecipazione.* (S. Marini, Ed.) Macerata: Quodlibet.

De Certeau, M. (1984). *The practice of Everyday Life.* Berkley, USA: University of California Press.

Education Youth Culture and Sport Council. (November 26, 2014). *Draft Conclusions of the Council and of the Representative of the Government of the Member States, meeting within the Council, on a Work Plan for Culture (2015-2018) - Adoption.* 15319/14 CULT 126 AUDIO 66 MI 869 RELEX 907 STATIS 121, Brussels.

Elena, O. (2013). Zone di comfort. Lo spazio pubblico nella città della differenza Milano. *Archivio di Studi Urbani e Regionali, Vol. 107/2013,* 9-29.

European Commission . (September, 9, 2005). *A Common agenda for Integration Framework for the Integration of Third-Country Nationals in the European Union .* Brussels.

European Commission. (2005). *Communication from the Commission to the Council, the European Parliament, the European Economic and Social committee and the Committee of the Regions - A Common Agenda for Integration - Framework for the Integration of Third-Country Nationals in the European Union.* COM (2005) 389 final, Brussels.

European Commission. (2008). *Communication from the Commission to the European Parliament, the Council, the European Economic and Social Committee and the Committee of the Regions of 17 June 2008 – A Common Immigration Policy for Europe: Principles, actions and tools.* COM (2008) 359 final , Brussels.

European Union, P. O. (2017). *How culture and the arts can promote intercultual dialogue in the context of the migratory and refugee crisis.* Luxembourg .

Foster, S. R., & Iaione, C. (2016). *The City as a Commons.* YALE LAW & POLICY REVIEW.

Gehl, J. (2010). *Cities for People.* Washington, USA: Island Press.

Hardin, G. (1968). the Tragedy of the Commons. *Science, New Series , 162* (3859), 1243-1248.

Harvey, D. (2012). *Rebel Cities: From the Right to the City to the Urban Revolution.* London: Verso.

Jacobs, J. (1992). *The Death and Life of Great American Cities* (Edizione Originale: 1961, New York: Random House Inc. ed.). New York, USA: Vintage Books Edition.

Lefebvre, H. (2014). *Il diritto alla città* (Edizione Originale: 1968, Paris: Ed. du Seuil ed.). (A. Casaglia, Ed., & G. Morosato, Trans.) Perugia, IT: Ombre Corte.

Lefebvre, H. (1991). *The production of space.* Oxford, UK: Basil Blackwell Ltd.

Madanipour, A. (2003). *Public and private space of the city.* London, UK: Routledge.

Madanipour, A. (2005). Public Space of European Cities. *Nordic Journal of Architectural Research* , *18* (1), 7-16.

Norberg-Schultz, C. (1980). *Genius Loci: toward a phenomenology of architecture.* London: Academy Ed.

Ostrom, E. (1990). *Governing the Commons: The Evolution of Institutions for Collective Action.* Cambridge University Press.

Penninx, R. (Dicembre 10, 2014). Il governo dell'immigrazione nei piccoli comuni. *Conferenza Internazionale realizzata nell'ambito del Programma di Ricerca di Interesse Nazionale (Prin) "Piccoli comuni e coesione sociale. Politiche e pratiche urbane per l'inclusione sociale e spaziale degli immigrati"*, (pp. 14-33). Roma.

Powell, J. (2015, June 18). *What makes a commons? Cities and the concept of 'urban commons'.* From University of Glouchestershire: http://www.ccri.ac.uk/what-makes-a-commons-cities-and-the-concept-of-urban-commons/

Ragab Nora, M. E. (February 15, 2016). *Role of Culture and the Arts in the Integration of Refugees and Migrants Report.* Brussels: European Expert Network on Culture and Audiovisual (EENCA), commissioned by the European Commission to inform the work of this group.

Sebastiani, C. (2010). Politica: governo collettivo dei beni comuni. In F. Bottini, *Spazio Pubblico – Declino, Difesa, Riconquista* (pp. 235-243). Roma: Eddiesse.

TAM Associati (Ed.). (2016). *Taking Care: progettare per il bene comune – Catalogo Padiglione Italia de La Biennale di Venezia, XV Mostra internazionale di Architettura*. Padova, Italia: Becco Giallo.

Union, C. o. (November 19, 2004). *Press Release of 2618th Council Meeting Justice and Home Affairs*. 14615/04 (Presse 321), Brussels.

United Nations – Human Settlements Programme (UN-Habitat). (2009). *Planning Sustainable Cities: Policy Directions – Global Report on Human Settlments 2009*. Earthscan.

United Nations, D. o. (2017). *World Population Prospects: The 2017 Revision, Key Findings and Advance Tables*. Working Paper No. ESA/P/WP/248, 2017, New York .

Yiftachel, O. (1991, January). State Policies, land control, and an ethnic minority: the Arabs in the Galilee region, Israel. *Environment and Planning D Society and Space 9(3)* , 329-362.

FOR A CULTURE OF URBAN COMMONS
PRACTICES AND POLICIES

Verena Lenna and Michele Trimarchi

"It is in cities to a large extent where the powerless have left their imprint – cultural, economic, social: mostly in their own neighbourhoods, but eventually these can spread to a vaster urban zone as 'ethnic' food, music, therapies and more. But it is this possibility – the capacity to make a history, a culture and so much more – that is today threatened by the surge in large-scale corporate re-development of cities".

Saskia Sassen

Who owns our cities – and why this urban takeover should concern us all

206 Verena Lenna and Michele Trimarchi

1. Occupied spaces between reclamation and protest

Appeared around 2011, the Occupy Movement has brought the attention back on the occupation of public and privately-owned spaces[1] to
manifest dissent[2]. But occupations have a longer and wider history.
Among their noble ancestors are the London occupation led by Ger-
rard Winstanley in 1649, when the label 'squat' was created to describe
the illegal occupation of land on the part of peasants, and the Paris
anarchic actions led by Georges Cochon together with upholsterers
since 1912, eventually supported by creative artists and the press. In
that case the logic was based upon the symmetry between unoccupied
houses and homeless families.

Without any ambition to cover the wide variety of possibilities and
hybrid combinations, a distinction can be made as far as the purposes
of occupations and, symmetrically, the role of space are concerned. In
such a respect occupations are direct actions aimed either at claiming a space back, or at reinventing it given a state of abandonment or
misuse. This is the case of squatting. The 1950s and 1960s gave rise to
a diffused and organized movement of squatters in many European
Countries, bringing with them a combination of social battles and creative intuitions: the conflictual orientation leading to occupations was
fed by a fertile and innovative artistic and cultural action, and the oc-

---

1 Zuccotti Park, the first space occupied by Occupy Wall Street (OWS), is a privately-owned public space (POPS) in New York City. Concerning the history of these
spaces in New York City, see Kayden (2000). Concerning the controversial potential
of these spaces in New York City, see Smithsimon (2008) and Schmidt/Nemeth/
Botsford (2011). Maps and data showing the proliferation of privately owned public
spaces are multiplying: London, San Francisco, Toronto and New York City among
others. On the risks for a democratic society related to privatization and financialization of cities see Sassen (2014) and Sassen (2015).

2 In the specific case of OWS the protest, which started on September 17th,2011, was
carried out against the logic of the financialization, resulting in speculation and
dispossession of resources. It could not have been more effectively expressed than
through the physical occupation of a publicly used space, literally enacting the right
to the city.

cupied places started to be transformed in venues for cultural events. The 'squatters' widened the field of their action, and conquered the interest and the passion of other continents, spreading in Chile, Argentina, Brazil, Colombia, Venezuela, Mexico, US, Canada, Australia, India, Taiwan, Thailand among the others.

But occupations can also be organized to protest, by exploiting the public function or the socio-cultural, symbolic value of a given space to amplify the message and its political importance[3]. Disturbance is produced by suspending the regular functions with non-relevant activities. Notoriously in the late 1960s schools and universities have been often occupied by students carrying out some protests about either social and political issues on the one hand, or specific school controversies on the other[4]. Between the 1960s and our years many things have changed. While then it was part of a wider flow of protests affecting many layers of society and substantially related to class conflict and the growing awareness of labour condition of the working class which also students exhibited sympathy to, now it appears to pursue a much more detailed and specific orientation due to the perceived (and often real) distance between the formal rules and the actual weights of school dynamics[5].

---

3 See, for a critical analysis of the various interests and views at stake, Vitale (2007).

4 School and university occupations present common features across the world, also due to the inclination to replicate simple actions, limited time brackets, and formal declarations in order for occupiers to feel part of a wide – and possibly international – community, gaining strength and credibility in their fight aimed at combining material improvements in the premises with looser regulations in exams. The phenomenon has crossed some peak periods, at the end of the 1960s and 1970s, but also in the most recent years. See, among the most recent articles, Barbie Latza Nadeau, "In Italy, angry students occupy schools", The Daily Beast, 22 november 2012 ; Paula Alegria and Marcielly Moresco, "Occupy and resist! School occupations in Brazil", Open Democracy, 13 october 2017.

5 An eloquent example is the invitation to occupy schools on the part of the group of Parents of African American Students Studying Chinese, who point at: a) less access to challenging courses in high school; b) lower-paid and less experienced teachers;

Unavoidably the two purposes – the reclamation of a resource and the protest – often overlap. In the case of squats, for example, the reclamation of an empty building and the installation of a different *modus vivendi* imply a critique to the system that caused that state of abandonment. Discontent is expressed as exodus, to use the words of Negri and Hardt (2000): the creation of an alternative that tries to escape power and its mechanism of normalization. On the other hand, to occupy a privately owned public space equals an immediate reclamation of its function, while taking advantage of the symbolic setting to protest against the system at large. Protest is performed through reclamation of a park as a representation of what it should be: public space as a dimension for the construction of a public opinion, and where critique could be expressed.

The reactions to occupations have been of different kinds: from evictions to attempts of negotiation with the legal owner of the occupied spaces, to agreement aimed at finally transforming illegality in temporary, legally recognized occupations, often based on a careful evaluation of costs and benefits in society's perception and in urban governance[6]. In any case, only when either the noise was considered less bearable by the establishment, or the legal owners claimed their properties back, specific interventions led to the (often violent) eviction of occupiers or the end of any agreements. Also related to the political colour of local governments.

In this chapter we will specifically look at those occupations which aim at the reclamation of the city, where alternative forms of governance are often experimented as leisure or cultural activities, organized by the persons involved. These two dimensions in fact cannot be distinguished, as samples of alternative urbanisms. Are these occupations about the reclamation of the city or about the creation of different cultural agendas? In fact, what we argue is that those occupations

---

c) three times higher probability to be suspended or expelled from school when compared with white students. See paassc.com.

6 Vitale (2007).

and the activities through which they are performed are about the emersion of a different culture *tout court*: a culture of the urban commons. It is a culture recognizing the right and the capacity of doing on the part of individuals and collectives, taking the city as the object of a continuous and spontaneous re-creation, and the social construction as its main side effect. It is a culture which may survive despite and beyond the dismantlement of the occupations.

What is interesting, through the examples here explored, is that the resource is not reclaimed by acting on a legal level or through some form of administrative intervention, but by practicing and experimenting a different form of governance, based on the engagement of the involved communities. Little by little a vacant site or building are embedded in an alternative, site-specific, spontaneously crafted fabric of exchanges and reciprocities, of individual and collective actions and programs. It is a new life, urbanity being recreated on the base of a different approach to the making of things and of the city. It is in these terms that we will discuss about the occupations, suggesting that the reclamation of the city is not simply about the redefinition of public and private sovereignties, but it is also – and maybe most importantly – about the installation of a different attitude, of a culture of inhabiting à la Heidegger. The practices of urban commons examined below can be considered an expression of that attitude.

When it comes to our cities and the progressive loss of urbanity arising from the growing financialization and the processes of privatization, those practices, generated by the inhabitants and grounded at a microscale, seem to suggest a possible answer, reclaiming the fine grain of the urban fabric by practicing the right to govern it, by practicing the commons as a culture.

210 Verena Lenna and Michele Trimarchi

2. The tragedy of the city: neglect or dispossession?

Despite their heterogeneity occupations are the response to some neglected – either individual or social – need, on the part of either an
organized group or a spontaneous agglomeration of people who converge on some major view, not without conflicts and diverging interests. They provide occupiers with possibilities that they could not enjoy
otherwise: the basic need of an accommodation, the desire to share
creative activities, the intention to express opinions and views at loud
voice, the refusal of steady conventions covering inequalities and right
violations.

Quite often their emersion is the reaction to missing action on
the part of the public administration. It could be just ordinary maintenance to be missing, concerning buildings, a district or any other
public asset; they are actions whose timeliness could allow the local
administration to effectively adapt the management of resources and
regulations to emerging (and even unpredictable) needs, rather than
simply ignoring them. In the light of such an absence, occupation often proves a sort of last instance action on the part of those who evidently feel neglected by the urban strategy, or – worse – pay the price
of the absence of any strategies[7].

Such a missing ring in the social chain, where the urban palimpsest
and the resident community should develop within a consistent reciprocity[8], combining effectiveness of services and equality of opportunities, indicates an approach to urban administration as an ex-post
intervention able to deal with ordinary problems through regulation
or funding aimed at rescuing weak components of the urban community (either people or organizations) when their political weight could
generate unwanted dissent. Within a political economy conceptual

---

7 Although many occupations start by initiative of artists, looking for undetermined,
abandoned spaces where they can freely express themselves, in a later time they
could be reached by the *désaffiliés* – as Castel (1994) defines them – as marginalized
individuals because either in precarious conditions or in poverty.
8 See Trimarchi (2014).

grid[9], no action is suggested when the potential dissent is not considered sufficiently important. This may occur, for example, when there is no solid critical permeability among social groups, when interest bearers are almost invisible, when some specific urban area is not the residence of many local taxpayers.

This weakness of public action in urban management is generated by the awareness, on the part of local administrators, of the main features of voters' choice, which is strongly affected by short memory and narrow sight in adopting decisions in the only case when this is possible: elections. Since voters' decisions appear to be strongly influenced by public action carried out within specific areas where voters live and/or work, and close to the election date, the related need to concentrate visibility of public action in the last period of every electoral term makes it difficult for local public decision-makers to consider urban governance appealing: it may generate consent but in the long run, with the risk of passing it on next-term administrators[10].

To a long-lasting neglect on the part of municipal administrations, some specific decision aimed at changing the legal framework related to ownership and management is often combined. If Kunsthaus Tacheles[11] in Berlin was occupied after a long institutional absence, the impact of decay and some partial demolition, Teatro Valle[12] in Rome was suddenly subject to a change in property and management after the abolition of the Italian Theatre Authority (ETI, Ente Teatrale Italiano): the theatre was abandoned with no project aimed at future man-

---

9   See, among the others, Nordhaus, W.D. (1975), Struthers/Young (1989).
10 Buchanan/Tullock (1962).
11 The political and artistic implications of Tacheles occupation and closure are examined by Jones (2012).
12 Despite the intensive discussion and the diffused interest for the Teatro Valle Occupato as the experiment of a new approach to theatre management, its story was quite short due to the substantial indifference of the municipal administration towards any possible solutions that could have combined the urgency not to abandon such an important space on one hand, and the needs of a group of professionals otherwise crowded out by the cultural market on the other. See Carrone (2014).

agement, and a group of theatre professionals decided to occupy it in order for its activity to be granted some continuity. In this case the source of spontaneous reaction had been an abrupt dismissal rather than systematic neglect.

Occupy Wall Street[13] pointed at the intrusion of the corporate establishment on governmental decisions, resulting in a growing distance between the 99 percent of the population and a 1 percent detaining most of the wealth of the world[14]. A stable camp was created and day-and-night activity was carried out, until the eviction on the part of New York Police Department on November 15th, 2011. In response to the attacks of that day the message of the occupiers has been "You can't evict an idea whose time has come"[15]. The movement elicited twin actions in many parts of the world from Great Britain to India, Chile and Greece, and was somewhat associated to the 'Arab spring'.

In other cases the occupation movement rises as the reaction to some threatened or started action whereby the local public administration intends to change the legal and actual destination of a shared space in order for its transformation to lead to a different use of public facilities. It was the case of Gezi Park in Taksim Square, Istanbul, where the public area devoted to shared leisure time was the object of a development plan. Protesters exploited this occurrence to extend the issues to many controversial changes in Turkish life and in the gradual weakening of the secularism which the Republic had been founded upon. Spread in other areas in the Country, the Gezi Park protest movement appears to have involved more than three million citizens (the official figures are much lower), and the final eviction ended with

---

13 The complex nature of the Occupy Wall Street movement, and the ambiguous ebollition of conflicting interests are focused, among the others, by Gautney (2011), and White (2017).

14 In 2017 Oxfam calculated that the 1 percent detained 82 percent of the wealth created in the world. See https://www.oxfam.org/en/pressroom/pressreleases/2018-01-22/richest-1-percent-bagged-82-percent-wealth-created-last-year

15 See Smucker et al. (2011).

eleven killed and more than 8000 wounded protesters; more than 3000 occupiers were arrested.

3. From 'Occupy' to the Urban Commons

Any occupation implies organization: for a couple of days or for several weeks, to make sure that food can be distributed and basic needs can be fulfilled, as in Gezi Park or at Zuccotti Park; to organize so that the just reclaimed resource could be protected and managed more efficiently or simply differently, as in Rome with Teatro Valle. What is interesting to observe is that the re-appropriation of neglected or misused urban spaces allows to experiment alternative uses and forms of organization. In fact, in the mentioned cases the establishment of an alternative governance of the reclaimed resource is the ultimate purpose, especially after the crisis of 2008, as an exasperated reaction to the inability of both the public and the private to manage resources.

What is being reclaimed is not only a building or a square, but also the ability of the involved community to take care of it, and to protect it, together with the right to decide about it, a right which is expressed as (and at the same time is further legitimized by) the capacity of managing the resource. In other words, what many occupations establish are practices of commoning. In fact according to De Angelis and Stavrides (An Architektur, 2010) – among many others[16] – three elements define the commons: a pool of common resources, a set of commoners estab-

---

16 In this chapter it is not possible to reconstruct the still open, large debate concerning the definition of the commons, in fact varying across the countries in relation to different cultural backgrounds, disciplinary frameworks and issues at stake. The definition of De Angelis and Stavrides looks adequate as it allows to seize the complexity of commoning as a process – beyond the definition of the commons as naturally given resources – and its capacity to continuously reproduce and evolve as a social construction, involving a variety of actors, balancing regulation and generativity.

lishing the rules to take care of those resources, and a process of commoning to create and reproduce the commons[17].

As very well known, the discourse of the commons is not new. It goes back to the Magna Charta[18]. Dramatically reduced by the enclosures, shared uses of the commons survived especially in less urbanized, peripheral contexts, such as small mountain communities, as showed by the jurist Paolo Grossi (Rosboch, 2015) with reference to the Italian experience. Ostrom (1990) specifically dealt with the governance of natural resources. But, as Mattei (2011) pointed out, the discourse on the commons powerfully (re)emerged in relation to occupations and urban settings, especially after the crisis of 2008, as an answer to the austerity regimes and as an alternative to the neoliberal management of resources.

Indeed in New York City the discourse was consciously adopted and a reflection on the commons started at the beginning of 2012, at the core of the activities of the collective Making Worlds[19]. Concerning Gezi, while chronicles of those days report that "a specific kind of urban participation and collaboration is gradually being established in the park"[20], the discourse of the commons was well known, and Istanbul was in fact one of the cities on the platform of Mapping the Commons[21].

Less noisy than the case of New York and Istanbul – perhaps because of a different symbolic, economic, cultural framework and of a different chain of events – in the same years a variety of occupations and forms of commoning started to proliferate. While continuing the

---

17 See the interview to De Angelis and Stavrides in AnArchitektur (2010)
18 See Linebaugh (2008).
19 To which Verena Lenna, co-author of this chapter, took part while living in New York City during the first half of 2012.
20 As reported in https://www.dinamopress.it/news/taksim-square-and-gezi-park-occupation-practicing-commons/
21 See the webpage dedicated to Istanbul, where the activities organized by Mapping the Commons are described, occurring during the days of the manifestations in November 2012. http://mappingthecommons.net/en/istanbul/

same discourse of the 'Occupy' movement, but having the chance of a longer (since less disturbing) permanence, they emerged especially in more densely urbanized contexts, increasingly at risk because of privatization and in the worst cases because of the financialization of the city, from community gardens to abandoned theatres, from empty buildings to airports. Although not corresponding to an unequivocal definition, the expression 'urban commons' is used in the scientific literature at the very least to refer to an urban setting and to distinguish these generative practices – as we shall see – from the natural, given commons such as air, water, land, and from those commons whose existence does not depend on any specific location and setting, such as intangible cultural heritage, the digital commons, seeds, just to mention a few[22].

Despite the number of variations, these practices – notoriously by now – suggest an alternative approach to managing resources, based on a shared definition of rules, on an attitude of care, on the direct engagement of the concerned communities. As a result the resource should be protected, while and because remaining accessible and available to a multiplicity of concerned communities, fulfilling their rights and their desires. In the next paragraphs we will shortly mention a few examples which might facilitate a more concrete understanding of the kind of activities and the values at the core of urban commons. In particular, we will take into consideration those practices of commoning performed as leisure activities, art or cultural projects[23].

---

22 This definition is proposed on the basis of a self-evident difference of the practices here considered from natural commons, hence allowing to take into account the specific conditions in which urban commons are established. In fact while the natural commons are given, the urban commons are the result of a spontaneous, continuous creation. While a critical review of that definition will be possible on the basis of a specific research hypothesis, for the purpose of this chapter we chose to align with the prevailing, quite homogeneous, understanding of the urban commons in the scientific literature. Among others, variations of that definition can be found in Ferguson (2014), Borch and Kornberger (2015), Dellenbaugh et al. (2015).

23 The cases here considered are only a few among many others, in general and in relation to the leisure and cultural activities oriented commons in particular. They

a) Kunsthaus Tacheles, Berlin

As a precursor of the forms of occupation here described, the case of Tacheles was established around twenty years before the 'Occupy' movement. It is mentioned here to suggest that alternative forms and settings for art and culture making have deep-seated roots. Present circumstances are probably finally providing us with a fertile ground for their multiplication. Almost twenty years after Christiania[24] a neglected building located in Berlin Mitte was occupied by some groups of creative artists who transformed the partially demolished place into a social centre and a sort of hub for contemporary art and antagonist culture. Also in the case of Kunsthaus Tacheles the story of the occupied space passed across many waves of uncertainty, from the project aimed at completely demolishing it to the intervention of a developer whose aim was to requalify the area with its likely fallout of gentrification. Born spontaneously just after the fall of the Berlin Wall in 1988, Tacheles aimed at giving voice to creative artists, as a reaction to the censorship-oriented DDR policy (Rost and Gries, 1992). Visited by Berliners and international travellers, Tacheles was dragged in legal con-

---

have been chosen on the basis of the direct engagement or personal knowledge of the authors, with no ambition to be exhaustive or representative. Together with other cases of occupations mentioned in this chapter these cases are taken from urban settings of developed Countries, belonging to the European context in particular, and experiencing similar economic transformations, although with differences. Other cases, from other Continents and Countries – besides a dedicated, specific research framework and means – would require to be situated on the background of very different economic, political and cultural circumstances, going beyond the ambitions and the actual purpose of this chapter. The information concerning these cases, when not deriving from a direct experience or contact of the authors with the collectives, are retrieved from the web (articles, blogs, official websites). The quoted sentences are taken from the official websites of each examined organization.

24 Founded in 1971 by a group of hippies who occupied an abandoned naval base (Lauritsen, 2002), Christiania was formally acknowledged as a self-managed urban area. After various and uncertain interactions between the community and the Danish government, and agreement has been reached in 2011: the residents will gradually buy the land due to a specific fund.

troversies, being cleared, then reopened, then closed, until September 2012, when its community was definitely evicted. Its activity was versatile: not only art production and exhibitions, but also concerts, dance performances and other forms of art were hosted by the cosmopolitan community located in Tacheles, although its connections with the urban grid were not extensively fertile; actually it was known and used by the art milieu, but the urban community was not involved in its life[25]. Tacheles appears as a case of thematic occupation, with its powerful attractiveness towards the art world, and its symmetrical absence from the urban community's point of view.

b) Teatro Valle, Rome

In 2010 the Italian government dismissed the Ente Teatrale Italiano (Italian Theatre Authority), a public agency active in theatre production and distribution, within a wider program of budget cuts. The historical Teatro Valle in Rome, a monument built in 1726, was abandoned, and the realistic option seemed to be its privatization (Povoledo, 2011). A group of theatre professionals, including actors, directors, technicians and musicians, occupied the Teatro Valle in June 2011 to avoid the legal passage to private owners and managers, and to craft professional opportunities that otherwise would have proved difficult. The three-years self-management season appeared to have broken a few conventions, since from Italy and from abroad many theatrical companies agreed to 'donate' their works to the 'Teatro Valle Occupato' (how it started to label itself); in the meanwhile the occupiers decided to transform their informal container into a foundation, and hired a group of experts – among whom the prominent jurist Stefano Rodotà – to write their statute, a wishful document based upon assembly decisions, managers' short-time turnout and a sort of improper use of the label 'common', although no real approach to the culture of commons was actually present in the internal regulations. The strategic aim was to use the foundation as a sort of Trojan Horse in order for political

---

25 See, on the controversies related to Tacheles, Donelli/Trimarchi (2019).

issues to be pursued through cultural action. In 2014 the legal property
of Teatro Valle passed from the Italian Republic to the Municipality of
Rome, and the occupiers left the theatre. Apparently there is a project
of rehabilitation of the building, although no theatrical and cultural
strategy is still visible. The long and uncertain times for bureaucratic
procedures leaves the (no more occupied) Teatro Valle in an institutional limbo whose outcome is still unpredictable.

c) Macao, Milan

"The real challenge is not to reproduce what you find in the market".
This, and other similar statements, define the search for a new identity and orientation collectively crafted during the occupation of Torre
Galfa in Milan on the part of the collective Macao. A wide community
of thirty- to forty-years old professionals active in various areas devoted their energy and creativity to Macao after a working day, aiming to craft a new cultural and social structure to face the future: "We
only ask to undermine your mode and to join us in order to try and
modify your model together with us". Romantic and trustful, Macao
refused any direct relationships with public institutions, while developing connections with grass-root associations, district committees,
universities. The Macao collective started its urban action in May 2012,
when an abandoned skyscraper was occupied by around two hundred
people led by the group 'Art Professionals', unwrapping the banner
"We could also think we can fly" (Demurtas, 2013). The strategic aim
of Macao clearly was to rethink life, work, relationships, and culture,
being aware of the powerful symbolic value that such an interrogative
approach to many urban certainties could be offered to the resident
community and its institutions. After eighteen months, in which two
evictions were carried out, Macao moved to the former slaughterhouse,
an abandoned liberty building where the ambitious project aims at
offering a new cultural system, a new museum, a library and above
all the space for cultural projects with no managerial rules. This can
be considered an experiment on action within a cultural commons
framework, where the informality and the absence of institutional re-

lationships (Macao even refuses the participation to public calls) may grant the shared responsibility and the cross-fertilization that represent the fundamentals of cultural commons.

d) Commons Josaphat, Bruxelles

"*L'utopie commence où la volonté politique s'arrête*". Shorter than a manifesto, sharper than a program. Commons Josaphat is a *collectif à geometrie variable*, a platform of individuals and associations, militants and inhabitants, established at the end of 2012 with the objective to propose an alternative development for the vacant site of Josaphat, based on the concept of the Commons. The shared resource is a 24 hectares' vacant site at the core of Brussels, situated between the municipalities of Evere and Schaerbeek. The site was formerly a marshalling yard. Today it belongs to the SAU (Société d'Aménagement Urbain), a company under public law whose majority shareholder is the Brussels-Capital Region and whose main mission is the implementation of development plans in strategic areas defined by the Region. Around and on the site, Commons Josaphat organized a variety of activities: from temporary, light or mobile installations to a collectively conceived manifesto for the development of the area, from picnics to the design of an *îlot modèle* – a prototype of an urban block conceived according to the principles of the Commons. For a long time abandoned and despite many projects – which could not be developed, given the entity of the site – the site is finally the object of a new Masterplan. The first proposal has been presented at the end of 2015 and citizens have been finally called to evaluate its latest version in June 2018, disappointing a large group of associations and inhabitants for the exclusive modalities of the process. Through all the years the purpose of Commons Josaphat, maintaining a non-conflictual attitude, has been to negotiate with the owners of the site a development based on a substantial involvement of residents, on the perpetual protection of land accessibility and of its ecological value. In a city which is demographically growing and which cannot expand beyond its regional borders, land is indeed a scarce resource and the site of Josaphat is one of the last *Zones d'Intérêt Regional*, the land reserves of the Region of Brussels. Adopting the claim "In case of emergency make your own city", associated with the icon of a shovel, Commons Josaphat points at a consistent and empowering implication of inhabitants in the making of the city, at the protection of the city as a commons, as a collectively and continuously regenerated opus whose primary purpose should be to give a solid answer to the basic needs of its inhabitants, resisting to any form of dispossession.

f) Campo de Cebada, Madrid

Created 'for' and 'by' the neighbours (*"por y para los vecinos"*) after the demolition of a swimming pool in the Latina district of Madrid, also the occupation of Campo de Cebada is a collective reaction against controversial orientations on the part of the local public administration. In such a specific case emphasis has been placed upon a further source of conflict: the symmetrical denial vs. acknowledgement of complexity in urban areas management; while potential conflicts are often dealt with from a static and even passive perspective, Campo de Cebada chooses to "inhabit conflicts" rather than eliminating them. In such a way the issues related to urban management are faced in a constructive way, rethinking their dynamics in order for a consistent rehabilitation process to be started and carried out no more occasionally and unevenly. Complexity can be managed and become a fertile feature to craft innovative shared protocols for decision-making and action; open processes are identified as the most effective solutions to positively live in a complex ecosystem. Also in the Madrid experience occupiers do not plan and act in conflict against public institutions; rather, they keep an open channel in order for the urban community (what they define "the citizenship") to interact with the urban administration, aiming to facilitate the participated construction of the city. The nature of commons is made ordinary through artistic and cultural events, and the multifold nature of the area, where specific initiatives smoothly coexist with individual and collective uses of the spaces, within a very loose time grid: cultural commons prove pluralistic by definition.

g) A Linha, Lisbon

The project 'A Linha' appears to be a more delicate and complex approach to urban life, in some way substituting the sum-of-individuals logic of conventional tourism with a more fertile shared use of (totally or partially) idle urban areas. In such a case the occupation is not focused on a specific and controversial area, but potentially spread in urban spaces where different uses could be imagined but they are not yet facilitated, encouraged or simply allowed. The 'Atelier Urban Nomads' label clearly identifies the strategic orientation of 'A Linha', whose philosophy is based upon re-appropriation of urban spaces in order for them to be made dynamic through city planning projects. Its main focus is on art, architecture and design, generating informal, playful and participative projects that can be finely tuned to contingent needs and desires. Within such a framework a part of the project is devoted at designing routes "not for tourists but essentially for inhabitants". Routes are the location of events, and residents are encouraged to "be the authors of their projects, not just to be consumers, to inspire a sense of responsibility, of concern and maintenance". Also in this experience the commons approach is evident, combining multiple and versatile uses of urban areas together with cultural visions, social capital and civic responsibility within a socially and culturally heterogeneous urban community.

h) Tempelhof Airport, Berlin

Almost five thousands apartments and commercial spaces, and a public library were at the centre of the project elaborated and proposed in 2014 by the Berlin municipal administration to develop the former Tempelhof Airport site, almost the size of New York City's Central Park. The development was planned on a publicly owned area, therefore the buildings should have been realized by state-owned housing companies. A clear majority of Berliners was decidedly contrary to such a project, and almost 65% of the voters gave their convinced support to the '100 percent Tempelhof Feld', rejecting the option according to which social housing in Berlin should have relied upon Tempelhof, in such a way subtracting a still empty and idle public area to shared and active enjoyment (gardening, riding bikes, playing football, picnicking, and the like). A sum of private benefits was clearly crowded out by the product of multiple desires aimed at the re-appropiation of a common space. In these cases the maps of urban commons and cultural commons extensively coincide. In any case the dilemma about social housing and the use of vacant spaces appears to be closely associated with another crucial dilemma: how to progressively involve citizens in public decisions and actions? Also from this point of view a commons approach can provide both dilemmas with a credible and possibly sustainable strategic orientation.

i) La Cavallerizza, Turin

In 1997 La Cavallerizza (a horse riding school) in Turin was included in the UNESCO world heritage list. In 2014 a group of residents reacted to the institutional threat to transform it into a private space also containing a youth hostel and other private businesses. 'Unreal Cavallerizza' is the project aimed at intensively using the space on the part of the urban community together with creative artists in order for participative cultural projects to craft a civic identity. Again, the commons approach emphasizes the multiple and shared use of urban spaces overcoming the static and slow institutional destinations, and at the same time rejecting the abuse on the part of privately oriented projects. Before engaging in a sort of ethical and political controversies, we should consider that the core of the problem is generated by the evident mismatch between neglected infrastructure on one hand, and weak civic participation on the other; it is clear that such a mismatch can erupt into conflict when ignored and left boiling for too long time. The good news, in Turin's case, is that after two years of creative occupation the municipal administration acknowledged the value of research, experimentation and proposal carried out by the occupiers, and asked them to elaborate a civic governance project, also declaring the commitment to raise the needed financial resources to fully give La Cavallerizza back to the citizenship. Just good intentions, so far, but an

encouraging starting point towards a possible institutional coopera-
tion between the urban community and the municipal administration.
The previously described re-appropriations interweave cultural
and spatial forms of interventions, suggesting unforeseen occasions to
reclaim the city and urbanity. Organized as urban commons, their side
effect is a process of social construction: an answer to *désaffiliation*[26]
and to the destabilizing dynamics of a liquid society, as Bauman (2000)
would define it. In all of them space is a resource, an opportunity, a
way of becoming. Either at risk of privatization or neglected, spatial
resources are reclaimed through cultural activities, by experimenting
alternative forms of governance. They are the theatre of a variety of initiatives which trigger the redesign of the existing institutional framework, as a result of the negotiations required for their realization between the administrative actors and the urban community. If on the
one hand they could have been fuelled and provoked by the previously
mentioned administrative inefficiencies, on the other hand they seem
to reveal that some more radical, deep-seated change is at stake.

A system of values is recognizable, despite the diversities, emerging
since the times of Tacheles and probably even before[27]: a desire of individuals and collectives to express themselves, while taking part to the
making of their living environment, to the preservation of resources
and of their accessibility to multiple communities of users, fuelled by
a forgotten sense of civic responsibility. A culture of the commons: we
suggest this expression in order to identify a *modus vivendi*, a change

---

26 See Castel and Haroche (2001).

27 *Le droit à la ville* by Henri Lefebvre was published in 1968, at the peak of the season
of students disputes. It was about the possibility of taking part to the making of
the city, as *oeuvre*, because *l'urbain se fonde sur la valeur d'usage*. The book served as
the foundation of the discourse on a substantial and empowering participation
in urbanism, situated at the top of the ladder of participation of Arnstein (1969).
In 1972 *An Architecture of Participation* was published, collecting the reflections of
Giancarlo De Carlo on the matter, following the season of students' occupations
and the related reflections concerning the role of the architect and a different approach to the architectural project.

that is pervasive and which in fact concerns many others domains, not considered in this chapter. Commons-oriented initiatives in fact are multiplying and covering a variety of needs: from housing to mobility, from education to food production, not without ideological ambiguities and the risks of co-optation, as Federici and Caffentzis (2013) point out[28]. They manifest the need and the desire to take action, as we shall see in next paragraph.

The commons are generative, generativity being about the ability to respond to scarcity with a creative approach, and about the ability of humans and non-humans to organize and co-operate between the protection of given resources and the elaboration of alternative uses of the existing resources, or the creation of new resources *tout court*. Generativity, recovering the original meaning of the word as meant by Husserl –*generativität* – is about life, about becoming and the generation of possibilities[29], as well as their emersion and across generations.

In other words, the commons are about the possibility of a continuous invention, about the (right to) continuous (re)creation of resources, meanings, tools and contents, in evolution with the changing characteristics of the involved communities and of their environment, according to the desire of individuals and collectives to become. To point

---

28 The word and the concept of sharing for example, isolated from the bundle of other values and principles at the core of the philosophy of the commons, has become a commons-friendly adjective to define activities which in fact are far from the concept of the commons. Uber and Airbnb are examples of the so called sharing economy.

29 Very shortly, we remind here that the concept of generativity came back to the attention of academia in 1995, with the book of Steinbock *Home and Beyond: Generative Phenomenology after Husserl*. In 2012 Marjorie Kelly in the book *Owning our future*, explores the generative forms of ownership, that is to say those forms of property creating the conditions favourable for the life of many generations to come. Ugo Mattei explicitly referred to this concept to describe the commons the first time in 2013, and later in 2015 in his work with Fritjof Capra, *The Ecology of Law. Toward a Legal System in Tune with Nature and Community*. More recently, in 2016 Serge Gutwirth and Isabelle Stengers deal with the concept of *générativité* in *Le droit à l'épreuve de la résurgence des commons*.

out the emergence of a culture of the commons has the main purpose to recognize this sort of paradigm shift, thus questioning under which conditions it could flourish, without forgetting the lesson of Boltanski and Chiapello (1999) about the risks of normalization and corruption of the original values, moving from practices to policies.

4. Loyalty, voice, exit? Action, possibly

The range of individual and social responses to managerial inadequacy was analyzed by Hirschman (1972) with reference to companies, organizations and public administrations, and has been extensively studied within the political economy textbook wisdom. The (individual or collective) perception of a sound decision-making body and of the related effectiveness of action leads people to simply adhere to the conventional rules, whether they are formally stated or informally acted. It is loyalty.

A more eloquent reaction consists in openly conveying a message to the decision-maker, declaring own dissent against some specific decision or action. It is voice, and it has been evolving using advanced – and possibly quick – tools such as letters, faxes, emails, twitter or facebook posts: this generates a bandwagon effect due to the possibility for the many to add their voice, in a technologically accessible and financially indifferent way. Voice can also be conveyed towards the decision maker through initiatives started by workers and then extended to many social layers, such as sit-ins, pickets, parades and the like, awarely introducing the risk of some material conflict between protesters and public order forces.

In Hirschman's analysis the extreme response is exit. It is a private reaction consisting in the material change of location on the part of citizens who find some feature of local administration unbearably expensive or engaging. It can apply to State legislation, and has shaming examples in the thousands of Jewish citizens who could not bear the weight of having been excluded by social, cultural and economic life; it can also apply to single individuals or families opting for a less heavy tax burden (such as the many retired persons who move to some 'tax favourable' Countries), and to individuals or families moving to avoid obstacles and blocks against access to the market labour. Loyalty, voice, and exit prove effective reactions to decisions and actions ranging from inadequacy to injustice. These appear to affect individual – and eventually social – life in some specific aspects such as labour regulations, tax regimes, political choices.

In some cases, many of which are described above, the inadequacy of public decision-makers and administrators can elicit a more complex reaction whose features do not limit to protesting and dissenting, but show a proactive attitude aiming to reclaim resources and the rights related to their use. It is the case of the previously mentioned occupations, re-appropriating vacant buildings and sites through practices of care and co-creation, grounded on the responsibilization of the involved subjects. It is action, the action of inhabitants, empowering because proving their agency, though not without obstacles and failures. Not simply a noisy response to institutional inabilities and inefficiencies, but experiments in governance aiming at independence rather than accepting assistentialism, while in almost all cases triggering some sort of interaction with the administrative actors. Indeed, in the various experiences we can highlight some recurring features showing that, although unavoidably moved by specific dissent reasons, action is enabled by awareness, information and competence. Rather an advanced and sophisticated response to institutional inadequacy, framing democracy in proactive terms, beyond the limited options offered by the electoral rituals[30].

Scenes of a proactive and creative use of resources, occupations are the arenas to experiment new forms of governance, thus elaborat-

---

30 The prevailing weight of the electoral rite upon the more complex processes of a democracy may explain the present crisis of the democratic models, and the magmatic emersion of controversial attempts of direct democracy: the Brexit case is eloquent enough to elaborate more concistent ways to manage public decisions between the representatives' and the electors' layers.

ing alternative views of society, equality, rights; redefining the tools and actions that can keep communities consistently tied and engaged; crafting cultural orientations. Solidly based upon political reasons and views, their features and modalities hence cannot be simply considered protest, which is in fact being replaced with extrovert re-appropriations of the self, of the collective, of resources, as interweaving moments of the same process. Explorations of the possible, they should be rather considered as cultural laboratories. Culture being meant not as *an object* of a – public or private – production, but as a social construction, a doing, a way of living, an attitude: in this case inspired by the philosophy of the commons[31].

The culture of the commons certainly cannot pervade every box in the institutional grid, but can possibly play a role in those areas where formalistic rigidity may lock social permeability, substituting conventional protocols with spontaneously crafted action. The generativity characterizing the creation of the commons – previously mentioned – can be seen as the opportunity for institutional rearticulation, aimed at filling the gaps inadvertently or indifferently opened by a steady and self-reproducing establishment. In such a respect the needed rigidity of a legal framework in which responsibility and accountability are formally stated may prove inadequate to respond to a continuously transforming urban eco-system, potentially not devoid of the paradoxes and contradictions deriving from a non-planned evolution of the personal, social and institutional organization.

On the contrary, where institutional rigidity has been disrupted by civic proactivity, experiences of occupation are featured by public debates, festivals, movie projections, artistic creativity, community gardening, meal sharing and many others. A panoply of activities, interweaving and exchanging the roles of the public, the intimate and the collective. Hence on the one hand we may observe the spectacularization of the inhabiting patterns, an exposition of the intimate sides

---

31 For an extensive exploration of the various features of cultural commons see Bert-
    acchini/Bravo/ Marrelli/Santagata (2012).

of the collective, a sort of second private nature; on the other hand, the self-organized production of more conventional cultural formats, aimed at the – collective and/or individual – re-appropriation of doings currently being either produced outside and parachuted in the area, or institutionalized[32].

5. Reclaiming the fine grain of the urban fabric

It would be a simplification to state that all occupations result in urban commons; and that all urban commons imply an occupation: not necessarily organizing equals commoning; and not necessarily urban commons require an occupation. What binds them together – despite the differences – is the need to permanently reclaim a resource or to reconceive the way a function is provided, in times of withdrawal on the part of the public administrations, dismantlement of the existing welfare models and growing privatization[33].

By pointing at the emersion of a culture of the commons our purpose is to highlight the fact that if neglected/vacant sites and buildings are being reclaimed this is not only a matter of re-use, of functional transformation or the result of redefining public and private sovereignties, but rather the expression of a system of values, among which are care and responsibility towards resources, and a desire of proactivity as far as the transformations of one's own environment is concerned. It is the desire of being part of a creative process, beyond the logic of production and consumption. While on the one hand urban commons may first of all provide us with a pragmatic answer to many needs, at the same time contributing to build a fabric of reciprocities on the background of a growing precarity and wealth polarization, on

32 On the direct production of cultural activities on the part of public administrations see Antonucci/ Morea/Trimarchi (2017).

33 ... and the reason why in this chapter we introduce urban commons starting from occupations, bringing together the concerns of urbanisms and those of economics of culture.

the other hand they seem to go beyond urgency and beyond insurgency as expression of a *modus vivendi*, as culture.

The fact that the cases here considered are leisure-oriented and culture-making forms of commons allows us to observe that (to start with) the culture of the commons necessarily represents a turning point concerning the industry of culture. The conventional view of culture adopts an approach based upon formal and institutional assessments. This has been generated and strengthened after the late Eighteenth Century, when the rising bourgeoisie needed an identity and used archaeological remains to justify its power in the social imaginary. This generated the interpretation of culture as a list of objects endowed with such a formal quality as a positive value. In the recent years this label of 'culture' is being slowly but firmly offset by a more comprehensive definition aimed at emphasizing the appraisal features and therefore reconciling the anthropologic glossary (culture as a system of shared beliefs, values, customs, behaviours, and artefacts) and the economic toolbox (culture as the evolving outcome of the household production function *à la* Stigler and Becker[34]).

Secondly – and more pervasively – to make the hypothesis of a culture of the commons should have the same effect of recognizing the ineluctability of a new idea whose moment has come, as the occupiers of Zuccotti Park proudly stated. This idea in particular has the potential to reclaim the city starting from the inhabiting practices; starting from the capacity to take care of a common pool of resources and to manage them while giving the possibility to multiple communities of users to fulfil their needs or express their desires; starting from the micro-scale of a building or of a square[35], as catalyzers of larger transformative process which might have an impact at the scale of a whole

---

34 See Stigler and Becker (1977), who emphasize the process of addiction which each cultural consumer is gradually subject to.

35 On the power of the small scale see Merwood Salisbury/McGrath (2013) and *Small Urbanism*, issue 27 of the urbanism magazine MONU (October 2017).

neighbourhood or at the scale of the whole city, depending on the in-volved communities.

In other words, the city reclaimed starting from the fine grain of the urban commons and their ecologies, opposing the loss of urbanity that comes with dispossession and neglect. Even in those cases where the morphology of a scrambled egg drawn by Price[36] in 1982 might be recognized, potentially suggesting a horizontal distribution of central-ities and opportunities, an indifferent distribution of functions and economic activities, the cartographies of wealth distribution describe in fact a condition of growing wealth polarization and socio-spatial segregation, with sharp contrasts visible and measurable at the scale of the same neighbourhood.

On the background of similar conditions, community gardens and vacant buildings represent in fact the residual, fragmented spatial oc-casions around which a spontaneous urbanity could still be developed, resisting to further privatization, gentrification and financialization of the city. As Sassen (2014) pointed out, it is a phenomenon whose scale and characteristics have nothing to do with the forms of real es-tate speculation and privatization of the 1980s, and whose main effect is the loss of urbanity: the loss of the city as a place where everybody has the right to be, to begin with.

In such an evolutionary framework the mentioned urban com-mons declare the obsolescence of projects and actions based upon cul-ture as a product ('culture for the city', 'the city for culture'). In fact they suggest that culture is a doing, the making of the city as a commons, using urban space as the infrastructure of a civic project, featured by a regulated accessibility and by fertile reciprocities. In this perspec-tive administrative inefficiencies and inabilities may have offered a providential void: an opportunity to rearticulate the role of adminis-trations, by grounding it in this emerging culture of the commons. In that direction the challenge hence is to avoid to institutionalize and to normalize commoning processes and to preserve a free-zone where

---

36   See Jacobs (2011).

new cultures and approaches to the governance of resources would constantly be experimented, according to the specific evolving needs of the communities at stake.

6. A taxonomy of urban commons: features and contradictions

This chapter has been written as the beginning of a shared reflection, built in between the concerns of urbanism and economics of culture. Two distinct disciplinary domains, but in fact overlapping in substantial way when we consider that even in the worst case scenario, which is to say when culture is merely an object of consumption, culture has an impact as far as the design and the uses of urban space is concerned. The proliferation of urban commons, on the contrary, represents the best case scenario: after two centuries of special statute and isolation in ivory towers, the practice of the urban commons brings back culture to its anthropological statute. Practicing the commons is a *modus vivendi* which reclaims the city starting from everyday practices. Beyond protest, as we suggested, urban commons are about action. At the core of it we find values such as the desire to care about resources, to contribute to their governance, less in the spirit of voluntarism than triggered by agency, motivated by the sense of empowerment deriving from the ability and the possibility to organize and to take part to a larger social construction, and supported by a sense of responsibility and self-regulation, so that the relevant resources could be protected while being accessible to the involved communities.

   In fact, if there is an example showing how making culture may actually be a political act – political being meant in the sense of Mouffe (2005): transforming society – that would be the urban commons. Examples of what Oldenburg (1989) defined as third spaces, urban commons promise a re-appropriation of the city through micro-practices, organized at the scale of still available or abandoned sites, fragments of spontaneous urbanity resisting to privatization and speculation. While in the short term they could allow temporary explorations of alternative uses, re-imagining the city, testing the capacities of the inhabitants to take care of the existing and newly created resources, in the long term urban commons imply the ability to protect resources, as the result not of mere regulations but of bundles of uses which involve a number of communities and recognize their right to decide about these resources.

If larger scales might be a challenge in terms of the ability to appropriate and manage, small scale re-appropriations allow us to imagine a capillary multiplication of initiatives, reclaiming the city through an acupunctural approach, transforming the urban fabric incrementally in the name of a culture of the commons. At the core of it, generativity as the capacity of continuous re-creation, and the right of individuals and collectives to have a role in the making of their environment, implying the possibility to decide – and, symmetrically – their responsibilization, questioning their ability to continuously re-organise, to govern the resources so that their needs and desires could be fulfilled.

The taxonomy described in the figure below is an attempt to represent the irreducible variety of urban commons. We labeled it dysfunctional: rather than forcing classifications it should in fact disrupt the conventional categories and invite the reader to imagine the range of different situations in which commons-oriented action might arise; the hybridizations but also the contradictory and multivalent aspects of these continuously evolving organizations; their different transformative capacities depending on the (site-)specific conditions in which they emerge and they operate.

As culture-based strategies urban commons appear to be effectively oriented towards offsetting metropolitan conflicts, compensating inequalities with alternative forms of reciprocity and economies, widening the spectrum of access, empowering diverse layers of the resident community to cooperate and cross-fertilize actions. Although there is not yet a systematic analysis on such a crucial impact, urban commons are increasingly becoming popular also among public administrators, though still in a selective fashion. The glossary and some of the values at the core of the culture of the commons seem to have been largely appropriated.

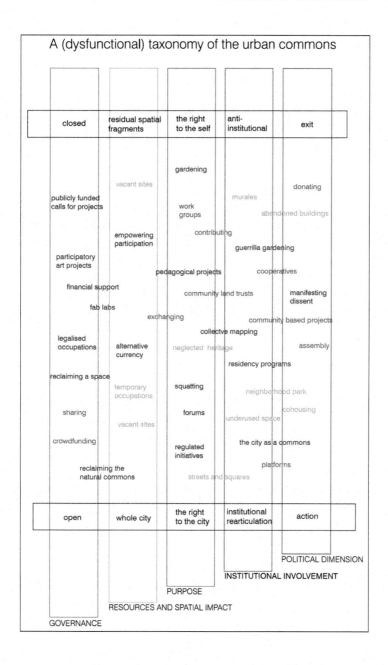

A (dysfunctional) taxonomy of the urban commons

A (dysfunctional) taxonomy of the urban commons. Every coloured element in the taxonomy is described by its colour and by its position with reference to the different dimensions defined by the columns. By imagining to move the element across the space of the taxonomy, different impact capacities and values are suggested. (graphics and concept by the authors)

The co-operative attitude – co-creating, co-working, co-housing and so on –, the power of sharing and caring, not to mention the word 'commons' in itself are mushrooming through administrative websites and calls for projects of any kind. More structurally, programs and regulations seemingly promoting the commons are also multiplying. In Bologna a regulation has been adopted in 2014 making the collaboration between citizens and the city possible. After that first case, in Italy 177 municipalities adopted a regulation for the governance of the commons and other 66 have started a procedure[37]. In Barcelona the model of the public commons is proposed at the base of the platform for participatory democracy *'decidim'*[38], established in 2015 and allowing citizens to propose and decide about their neighborhoods and city. In Lille the initiative *'Encommuns'* started to map and document the commons economy since 2015 and an *Assemblée des Communs* has been established since 2017. The city of Ghent commissioned a study on the emersion and the growth of the commons, with the purpose to elaborate indications for the implementation of supportive public policies[39].

But as previously mentioned, co-optation is a real threat to the emancipatory potential of the commons and contradictory attitudes of administrations seem to confirm this suspicion: more or less violent evictions are still perpetrated, thus abandoning the city in the hands of speculators and global corporations. It happened – paradoxically? – in Bologna, where the Labas occupation has been terminated despite the successful implantation of projects promoting local agriculture, chil-

---

37 As reported by Labsus, Laboratorio per la Sussidiarietà, http://www.labsus. org/i-regolamenti-per-lamministrazione-condivisa-dei-beni-comuni/

38 The platform can be accessed at https://decidim.org/

39 See Bauwens and Onzia (2017).

drens' activities and supporting migrants' rights[40]. In Rome, hundreds of abandoned buildings and heritage, since many years animated by the activities of local associations and collectives, risk to be evicted given the absence of a regulation on the commons[41].

In Brussels, despite the growth of the movement of (urban) commons and the increasing attention to the emerging forms of co-creation in the city, the regional administration is still hesitating to implement the project of an urban block as a commons in the site of Josaphat. In Berlin the 'Friedel 54' squat has been evacuated to leave the building to the new owner, a corporation based in Luxembourg, on the background of an increasingly gentrified and dispossessed city[42]. Many other examples could be mentioned. In fact privately owned public spaces are multiplying all over the world, as we mentioned at the beginning of this chapter, with dangerous implications concerning the rights and uses associated to these spaces, concerning democracy at large. Without forgetting – as an indicator of the overall climate – the number of battles communities all over the world still have to fight against real tragedies of the commons, happening when the involved communities do not have any power to decide about their rivers, their lands, their forests and other natural commons.

Hence, while it is important to recognise the signs of a still fragile rising culture of the commons, it is important to be vigilant and critical concerning these contradictory signs. If on the one hand a transition towards a commons-based society has been claimed as unavoidable[43], on the other hand neo-liberal dynamics are evidently still dominant

---

40 See Mattei (2017).

41 As reported in https://ilmanifesto.it/roma-il-regolamento-sui-beni-comuni-non-ce-e-la-giunta-desertifica-la-citta/

42 As reported here http://www.exberliner.com/features/zeitgeist/friedel54-s-last-stand/ among others.

43 On the transition towards a commons-based society see the work and research of Michel Bauwens, founder of the p2p Foundation and main contributor of the Commons Transition, on the website https://primer.commonstransition.org/. But also Rifkin (2014).

and in good health[44], legitimizing doubts about the capacity of a commons- based society to emerge and to thrive.

7. Concluding remarks: empowering the cultural turn of the urban commons

Having pointed at the emancipatory potential of urban commons both at an individual and at a collective level, learning from the practices we suggest that a problematization of the previously mentioned and other forthcoming policies is a necessary step to avoid co-optation and normalization. While the discourse on the commons possibly re-emerged and could have been appropriated on a large scale – directly or indirectly – thanks to the 'Occupy' movement, the proliferation of administrative tools and programs has only recently become more consistent. This is indeed a delicate moment as far as the empowerment of the urban commons is concerned. In the light of the mentioned contradictions a critical, vigilant posture should take into account the ability of capitalism to absorb and neutralize any form of alternative organization rising as a critique to the dominant discourse, as notoriously described by Boltanski and Chiapello (1999). This risk was also highlighted by Mattei (2013), who talked about the possibility of a *"détournement a contrario"* of the practices of commoning.

Having in mind what the urban commons are about, their origins and their potential in terms of re-appropriation of urbanity as part of a *modus vivendi*, learning from practices and their underlying values, our working hypothesis is that four criteria should be considered, with the

---

44 While on the one hand, especially after 2008, it has been said capitalism is not working, as the Occupy movement claimed and as Piketty (2013) proved with his work on increasing inequalities; on the other hand, *de facto*, inequalities and richness polarization are growing. Proving that despite its contradictions and *through* its contradictions, capitalism in its neoliberal version is still ruling the world. The privatization of public space, mirrored by the privatization of heritage and culture, is at the same time an effect and a means of the logic of financiarization.

purpose to problematize existing policies and for the establishment of new frameworks of governance:

a) The first is the role of the involved communities in the definition of those policies, programs and regulations, in the name of the right to decide reclaimed by the (urban) commons. Whenever these should be conceived solely at an administrative level, the risk would be to over-look the right to decide authentically implied in the practices of com-moning, considering them once again as the object of an external, reg-ulatory framework. The inclination for taking care and for assuming the responsibility concerning the governance of a given resource could only last if backed by a power to decide on the part of communities and individuals. It is a matter of protecting the resource which different uses and rights of those communities rely upon. But also – and per-haps most importantly – a matter of meaning and recognition, moti-vating the gratuitous actions of the commoners.

b) The second is the ability of those policies, programs and regula-tions to create favourable conditions to the mentioned generativity of the (urban) commons. While regulation might indeed "discipline the forms of collaboration between citizens and the administrations"[45], this does not necessarily equal the creation of a climate favoring the emersion of the urban commons, especially when in the same city where the regulations are established evictions are still practiced, rais-ing doubts about the actual purposes at the origin of those regulations. Urban commons – as distinct from natural commons – can be seen as inhabiting practices à la Heidegger, between the expression of the self and the social construction. Spontaneous and site-specific, they may certainly be encouraged by the existence of a regulatory framework,

---

45 As stated in the Bologna *Regolamento sulla collaborazione tra cittadini e amministra-zione per la cura e la rigenerazione dei beni comuni urbani.* Accessible at http://www.comune.bologna.it/sites/default/files/documenti/REGOLAMENTO%20BENI%20COMUNI.pdf

even more so in the case in which these regulations have been collectively defined. Similarly, calls for projects triggering the initiatives of the citizens and other programs may provide the urban community with a relevant contribution in terms of funding, visibility, and networking capacity. But on the other hand they could lead to competitiveness among different initiatives and/or continue to fuel forms of either visible or hidden assistentialism. In other words, the effect of the different administrative interventions and frameworks – singularly taken and as a whole – should be evaluated, between the risk of further fragmentation of efforts and resources on one hand and the possibility to nourish synergies and upscale transformations on the other hand, beyond the limits of the occupied building or vacant site.

c) The third element to consider in the design of institutional frameworks supporting urban commons should concern the actual ability of policies as such to empower an effective protection and governance of the resources at stake. In addition to policies and regulations, we believe that a further tool to be considered should be the project, urban and cultural at the same time. Given the unpredictable, transformative and mutable nature of the commons as site-specific, unique combinations of resources and actors, we consider – beyond policies and regulations – that the project as a trans-disciplinary process could allow the creation of synergies, of long-term strategies, operating on multiple levels at the same time, and connecting different forms of urban commons. If governance is paramount for the sustainability of the urban commons, the project – by virtue of its envisioning power – could be the process facilitating the encounter of different expertises, allowing to scale and to balance the abilities and responsibilities of the involved communities and actors with the characteristics of the concerned spatial resources and of the non-human[46].

---

46 Concerning the role of the project as a process of responsibilization see the forthcoming doctoral dissertation by Lenna (2019).

d) The fourth aspect to be questioned would be about the radicality of the transformation concerning the functioning of institutions and administrative frameworks, towards a commons-oriented society. How could they be transformed by the cultural turn of the commons, while supporting them? We imagine that an iterative logic is what would allow a continuous adaptation of policies and projects to the needs and characteristics of the emerging urban commons, by absorbing and amplifying their logic. This could happen – once again – making sure that the concerned communities could have a decisional role about policies and projects based on their practices, needs and expertises, between the right to manage resources and the responsibility that this implies.

On the basis of these elements we suggest that further research should be developed concerning the existing policies and the emerging approaches, with the purpose of investigating upon their ability to interpret and to contribute to the cultural turn expressed by the urban commons. In 1961 Cedric Price was asked by the theatre director Joan Littlewood to design a theatre as a flexible armature, capable of adapting to a variety of performances and uses, a laboratory for fun, able to be transformed according to any cultural program and to the desires of any kind of user.

The Fun Palace was designed as a very simple structure, allowing almost any kind of transformation, with very little constraints and already including the machineries required to move walls and other architectural elements across the volume. Should we suggest an image to describe the policies and institutional frameworks supporting the emergence and the proliferation of urban commons, it would be something very similar to the Fun Palace: a structure still necessary for practices to happen, but minimally defined and capable of continuously responding to the very life of those practices. Our magmatic society, in a stage of intensive mutation, needs to disrupt the conventional formats.

References

An Architektur (2010): "On the Commons: a public interview with Massimo De Angelis and Stravros Stravrides", An Architektur: On the Commons, 23.

Antonucci, F./Morea, V./Trimarchi, M. (2017): Public Decision-Making Processes for Cultural Projects: A Political Economy Perspective, in Proceedings of 6th Annual International Conference on Law, Regulations and Public Policy, Singapore: GSTF, pp. 109-12.

Arnstein, S.R. (1969): "A ladder of citizen participation", Journal of the American Planning Association, 35/4, pp. 216-24.

Baumann, Z. (2013): Liquid modernity, London: Routledge.

Bauwens, M./Onzia, Y. (2017): Commons Transitie Plan voor de stad Gent. In opdracht van de stad Gent. Retrieved from: https://tinyurl.com/ybyj5qd4.

Bertacchini, E./Bravo, G./Marrelli, M./Santagata, W. (2012, eds.): Cultural Commons. A New Perspective on the Production and Evolution of Cultures, Cheltenham: Edward Elgar.

Boltanski, L./Chiapello, E. (1999): Le nouvel esprit du capitalisme, Paris: Gallimard.

Borch, C./Kornberger, M. (2015, eds.): Urban commons: Rethinking the city, Abingdon, Routledge.

Buchanan, J.M./Tullock, G. (1962): The calculus of consent: logical foundations of constitutional democracy, Ann Arbor: Michigan University Press.

Carrone, I. (2014): "Quale futuro per il Valle Occupato?", Doppiozero, July 9th.

Castel, R. (1994): "La dynamique des processus de marginalisation: de la vulnérabilité à la désaffiliation", Cahiers de la recherche sociologique, 22, pp. 11-27.

Dellenbaugh, M. et al. (2015): Urban commons: Moving beyond state and market, Basel: Birkhäuser.

Demurtas, A. (2913): "Macao, I primi diciotto mesi del collettivo cultur-ale. A Milano si sperimenta un nuovo modo di fare cultura", Let-tera43, October 12th.

Donelli, C./Trimarchi, M. (2019): "Where is Berlin? Cultural commons and urban policy among real and virtual walls", forthcoming in Eu-ropean Journal of Creative Practices in Cities and Landscapes, 2.

Ferguson, F. (2014): Make_shift City. Renegotiating the urban com-mons, Berlin, Jovis.

Gautney, H. (2011): "What is Occupy Wall Street? The history of leader-less movements", The Washington Post, October 10th.

Hardin, G. (1968): "The tragedy of the commons", Science, 162, pp. 1243-48.

Heidegger, M. (1962): Being and Time (translated by Macquarrie, J./Robinson, E.), Oxford: Blackwell.

Hirschman, A.O. (1972): Exit, voice, and loyalty. Responses to decline in forms, organizations, and states, Boston: Harvard University Press.

Jacobs, F. (2011): The eggs of Price: an Ovo-Urban analogy, Big Think (bigthink.com).

Jones, J. (2012): "The closure of Berlin's Tacheles squat is a sad day for alternative art", The Guardian, September 5th.

Kayden, J.S. (2000): Privately owned public spaces. New York City Ex-perience, New York: John Wiley & Sons.

Lauritsen, P.W. (2002): Christiania, Copenhagen: Kirsten Corvinius.

Lenna V. (2019): The project of property as emancipation. A Communi-ty Land Trust in Brussels, forthcoming doctoral dissertation.

Linebaugh, P. (2008): The Magna Charta manifesto. Liberties and com-mons for all, Berkeley: University of California Press.

Mattei, U. (2011): Beni comuni. Un manifesto, Bari: Laterza.

Mattei, U. (2017): "L'occupazione dei beni comuni è vera politica", Il Fat-to Quotidiano, August 10th.

Merwood Salisbuty, J./McGrath, B. (2013, eds.): Scapes 8: Triggers: Ur-ban design at the small scale, New York: CreateSpace.

Negri, A./Hardt, M. (2000): Empire, Harvard: Harvard University Press.

Nordhaus, W.D. (1975): "The political business cycle", The review of economic studies, 42/2, pp. 169-90.

Ostrom, E. (1990): Governing the commons: The evolution of institutions for collective action, Cambridge: Cambridge University Press.

Piketty, T. (2013): The economics of inequality, Harvard: Harvard University Press.

Povoledo, E. (2011): "Outrage over a storied Roman theater's future", The New York Times, June 27th.

Rifkin, J. (2014): The zero marginal cost society: The internet of things, the collaborative commons, and the eclipse of capitalism, London: Palgrave Macmillan.

Rosboch, M. (2015, ed.): Paolo Grossi. Le comunità intermedie tra moderno e pos-moderno, Torino: Marietti 1820.

Rost, A./Gries, A. (1992): Berlin, Berlin: Elefanten Press.

Sassen, S. (2014): Expulsions. Brutality and Complexity in the global economy, Harvard: Harvard Univeristy Press.

Sassen, S. (2015): "Who owns our cities – and why this urban takeover should concern us all", The Guardian, november 24th.

Schmidt, S./Nemeth, J/Botsford, E. (2011): The evolution of privately owned public spaces in New York City, Urban Design International, 16/4, pp. 270-84

Smithsimon, G. (2008): "Sunset in the imperial city: how New York's public spaces presage the end of Empire, Journal of Aesthetics and Protest, 6, pp: 230-44.

Smucker, J.M./Manski, R./Gaçuça, K./Palmer Paton, L.M./Holder, K./Jesse, W. (2011): "Occupy Wall Street: you can't evict an idea whose time has come", The Guardian, november 15th.

Stigler, G./Becker, G. (1977): "De gustibus non est disputandum", American Economic Review, 67/2, pp. 76-90.

Struthers, J./Yong, A. (1989): "Economics of voting: Theories and Evidence", Journal of Economic Studies, 16/5.

Trimarchi, M. (2014): Urbs et Civitas: una mappa della cultura, in De Biase, F. (ed.): I pubblici della cultura. Audience development, audience engagement, Milano: Angeli, pp. 138-50.

Vitale, T. (2007, ed.): In nome di chi? Partecipazione e rappresentanza nelle mobilitazioni locali, Milano: Angeli.

Weller, R. (2016): The city is not an egg: western urbanization in relation to changing conceptions of nature, in Stenier, F.R./ Thompson, G.F./Carbonell, A. (eds.): Nature and cities: the ecological imperative in urban design and planning, Cambridge MA: Lincoln Institute of Land Policy.

White, M. (2017): "I started Occupy Wall Street. Russia tried to co-opt me", The Guardian, November 2nd.

About the authors

Ottavio Amaro, PhD, Associate Professor of Architectonic and Urban Composition, "Mediterranea" University (Reggio Calabria, Italy)

Federica Antonucci, PhD candidate in Cultural Economics, "Mediterranea" University (Reggio Calabria, Italy) and KU (Leuven, Belgium)

Arthur Clay, founder and artistic director, Virtuale Switzerland (Basel, Switzerland)

Lidia Errante, PhD, "Mediterranea" University (Reggio Calabria, Italy)

Letteria G. Fassari, PhD, Professor of Sociology of Contemporary Cultures, "La Sapienza" University (Roma, Italy)

Verena Lenna, PhD candidate in Urbanism, IUAV (Venice) and KU (Leuven). Co-founder of Commons Josaphat (Bruxelles, Belgium)

Irene Litardi, PhD, Post-Doc fellow in Sustainability Management, "Tor Vergata" University (Roma, Italy)

Valeria Morea, PhD candidate in Cultural Economics, "Mediterranea" University (Reggio Calabria) and Erasmus University (Rotterdam). Economic Analyst, Tools for Culture (Roma, Italy)

Domenica Moscato, PhD, "Mediterranea" University (Reggio Calabria, Italy)

Lavinia Pastore, PhD, Post-Doc fellow in Management, "Tor Vergata" Unversity (Roma, Italy)

Clarissa Pelino, Urban School SciencesPo Paris. Manager of Urban Projects, Manifesto (Paris, France)

Tom Rankin, MArch, Architect and Professor of Architecture, California Polytechnic State University

Monika Rut, co-founder and communication manager, Virtuale Switzerland (Basel, Switzerland)

Marina Tornatora, PhD, Architect and Lecturer, "Mediterranea" University (Reggio Calabria, Italy)

Michele Trimarchi, PhD, Professor of Public Economics, "Magna Graecia" University of Catanzaro. Founder, Tools for Culture (Roma, Italy)

Printed by Printforce, United Kingdom